Let Your Light Shine:
A Guide for Preparing
to Teach in a Catholic School

CATHOLIC EDUCATION STUDIES DIVISION

Alliance for Catholic Education Press
at the University of Notre Dame

Let Your Light Shine:
A Guide for Preparing
to Teach in a Catholic School

by
Gail Mayotte, SASV

ALLIANCE FOR CATHOLIC EDUCATION PRESS
AT THE UNIVERSITY OF NOTRE DAME

Notre Dame, Indiana

Copyright © 2010

Alliance for Catholic Education Press
University of Notre Dame
158 I.E.I. Building
Notre Dame, IN 46556
http://www.nd.edu/~acepress

ISBN 978-1-935788-00-3

Cover design by Mary Jo Adams Kocovski
Text design by Julie Wernick Dallavis

"The Respectful Teacher" reprinted from *Prayers to Guide Teaching* by Gail Mayotte, SASV.
Copyright © 2007 Alliance for Catholic Education Press. Used by permission. All rights
reserved.

Library of Congress Cataloging-in-Publication Data

Mayotte, Gail.
 Let your light shine : a guide for preparing to teach in a catholic school / by Gail Mayotte, SASV.
    p. cm.
 Includes bibliographical references and index.
 Summary: "Offers background information for novice Catholic school teachers about areas to consider in
planning for the school year, practical suggestions and tips from teachers, and forms and templates ready for
use in the classroom"--Provided by publisher.
 ISBN 978-1-935788-00-3 (pbk. : alk. paper)
 1. Catholic teachers--Training of--United States. 2. Catholic schools--United States. 3. Catholic Church--
Education--United States. I. Title.
 LC501.M358 2010
 371.071'273--dc22
                              2010017770

This book was printed on acid-free paper.

Printed in the United States of America.

To the memory of Jeannette Beaudry, SASV,
who mentored me in my first year of Catholic school teaching.

Contents

Acknowledgments

My gratitude is extended to the editorial staff of ACE Press—Julie for her guidance, MJ for her graphics—and to Tom Doyle and Fr. Ron Nuzzi for their review of the book and valuable feedback.

Additionally, I wish to acknowledge the following alumni of the Alliance for Education program who accepted the invitation to share teaching tips or segments of their management plans: Anna Arias, Allison Astuno, Heather Barker, Noah Beacom, Michelle Blair, Amy Bozzo, Kathleen Burke, Katie Cawley, Anthony D'Agostino, Nick Dailey, Rory Dippold, C.J. Egalite, Laura Farrell, Meghan Finerghty, Lindsay Fitzpatrick, Lauren Flynn, Brett Guy, Matthew Houlihan, Brynn Johnson, Patrick Kaiser, Katie Key, Annie Walorski Morin, Clare Murphy, Maya Noronha, Michael O'Connor, Matt Reichert, Sarah Runger, Brendan Ryan, Maggie Schroeder, Courtney Jianas Vogtner, Patrick Vogtner, David Yeager. Their practical advice and creative ideas provide helpful suggestions and are greatly appreciated.

Preface

There are a variety of approaches in the discipline of education to teach teachers how to teach. From issues of classroom management to the details of content specific pedagogy, teacher educators face a challenging task. Our approach at the University of Notre Dame emanates from the lived experience of the Alliance for Catholic Education (ACE) Program, a two-year service through teaching program that welcomes recent college graduates into teaching. Each summer, a new cohort of ACE teachers begins their educational experiences with a course entitled, "Introduction to Teaching." This course, organized by Tom Doyle, Ph.D., Academic Director of the program, unfolds over a span of five days during which students engage in preparing a classroom management plan in preparation for their teaching in Catholic schools. Five essential areas are emphasized: the Catholic Classroom, Procedures and Routines, Rules and Consequences, Spending Classroom Time Well, and Grading and Parent Communication.

The origin of this book is in this weeklong course with each of its chapters addressing one of the five areas. Though originally framed by this course, its application is for anyone preparing to teach in a Catholic school. The book offers background information about important areas to consider in planning for the school year, practical suggestions and tips from teachers, and forms and templates ready for use. It additionally offers questions to consider in developing a classroom management plan. The framework of the book is such that it encourages revisiting as needed over the course of the academic year.

Introduction

Teachers hold tremendous responsibility for shaping the environment and learning experiences for their students. In Catholic schools, these responsibilities are strengthened and directed by the school's Catholic identity, the underlying foundation and purpose for the school's existence. In the Church document, *The Religious Dimension of Education in a Catholic School*, elements that distinguish the religious dimension of a Catholic school are enumerated: "a) the educational climate, b) the personal development of each student, c) the relationship established between culture and the Gospel, d) the illumination of all knowledge with the light of faith" (Congregation for Catholic Education [CCE], 1988, §1). Each of these areas constitutes an important avenue for shaping the environment and learning experiences for students. Whether focusing on teaching religion or teaching other subjects, whether interacting with students or communicating with their parents, whether outlining expectations or disciplining students, all choices and actions should flow from the school's Catholic identity.

Creating a management plan holds great value as a new teacher prepares to teach. It encourages critical and creative thought about forming a classroom community, organizing a productive learning environment, and shaping meaningful instructional experiences. Once written, it becomes a guide for beginning the school year. Resource books abound for new teachers to help with planning and organizing those early days. This resource differs in that it emphasizes Catholic identity elements as they influence areas for consideration in a classroom management plan.

Chapter 1, "The Catholic Classroom," reinforces the important elements of message, community, service, and worship. Chapter 2, "Routines and Procedures," encourages efficient use of class time for administrative tasks as well as responsible membership in the classroom community. Rules and consequences, the focus of chapter 3, promote the moral development of students and are supported by solid teacher-student relationships in which respect is the foundation. The focus of chapter 4 is spending classroom time well which depends on thorough planning that considers carefully not only curriculum expectations but the specific needs of the individual students the teacher is privileged to teach. The final chapter, "Grading and Communication," emphasizes communal relationships and supports parents in their roles as the primary educators of their children. Each of these areas is distinct in the responsibilities that it requires yet all remain connected in the big picture of a teacher's effectiveness as a Catholic school educator.

Each chapter is structured in a similar manner. A brief introduction is followed by the citation of some research that informs the topic. Considerations for planning in the given area are then discussed including examples of successful practices in action. Each chapter ends with tips from the field provided by former Alliance for Catholic Education (ACE) teachers, usable forms and templates, and questions to guide the creation of a management plan.

After reading each chapter, take time to reflect upon and write specific ideas and structures that you want to incorporate into your management plan. Doing so will develop a resource that will provide a valuable reference for setting up your classroom and for maintaining focus in the early days of the academic year.

In an address to Catholic educators during a visit to the United States, Pope Benedict XVI (2008) reminded of the importance that "public witness to the way of Christ, as found in the Gospel and upheld by the Church's Magisterium, shapes all aspects of an institution's life, both inside and outside the classroom." Thomas Groome (2001) writes about spirituality as the foundation for Catholic education noting that it "must permeate the whole curriculum of Catholic education—what and why, how and who we teach" (p. 68). Both of these messages highlight the important role of the classroom teacher in shaping a faith-filled learning environment for students. May faith inform your management plan so that students come to experience Christ in the learning environment you create.

REFERENCES

Benedict XVI. (2008, April). *Meeting with Catholic educators.* Retrieved July 28, 2009, from http://www. vatican.va/holy_father/benedict_xvi/speeches/2008/april/documents/hf_ben-xvi_spe_20080417_ cath-univ-washington_en.html

Congregation for Catholic Education. (1988). *The religious dimension of education in a Catholic school.* Washington, DC: United States Catholic Conference.

Groome, T. (2001). Building on a rock: A spiritual foundation for Catholic education. In C. Cimino, R. Haney, & J. O'Keefe (Eds.), *Catholic teacher recruitment and retention: Conversations in excellence* (pp. 63-74). Washington, DC: National Catholic Educational Association.

The Catholic Classroom

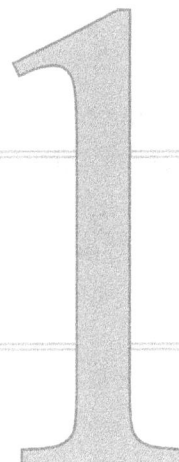

1

Every teacher in the Catholic school serves an important role in helping to animate the school's mission and Catholic identity. This critical and essential responsibility takes form as teachers give witness to their faith in word and action, a faith strengthened through prayer and nurtured in community.

Church documents such as *Renewing Our Commitment to Catholic Elementary and Secondary Schools in the Third Millennium* (United States Conference of Catholic Bishops [USCCB], 2005), *Lay Catholics in Schools: Witnesses to Faith* (Sacred Congregation for Catholic Education [SCCE], 1982), *The Catholic School on the Threshold of the Third Millennium* (Congregation for Catholic Education [CCE], 1997), and *The Religious Dimension of Education in a Catholic School* (CCE, 1988) provide rich sources of inspiration and insight for living one's call to serve as a Catholic School teacher. It is noted within this last document that the "prime responsibility for creating [the] unique Christian school climate rests with the teachers, as individuals and as a community" and that the religious dimension of the school "is expressed through the celebration of Christian values in Word and Sacrament, in individual behavior, in friendly and harmonious interpersonal relationships, and in a ready availability" (CCE, 1988, §26). These characteristics of the religious dimension which include qualities for meaningful interactions outline a simple guide for creating a Catholic culture for learning.

Furthermore, attention to the fourfold purpose of Christian education outlined by the United States bishops (2005) draws attention to concrete and necessary ways for attending to one's Catholic classroom, "to provide an atmosphere in which the Gospel message is proclaimed, community in Christ is experienced, service to our sisters and brothers is the norm, and thanksgiving and worship of our God is cultivated" (p. 1). Message, community, service, and thanksgiving are focal areas for the Catholic classroom and attention to each of these is essential.

WHAT RESEARCH SAYS

- Based upon the Holy See's Teaching on Catholic Schools, Archbishop Miller (2006) writes that there are five essential marks of a Catholic school: the school is "inspired by a supernatural vision, founded on a Christian anthropology, animated by communion and community, imbued with a Catholic worldview throughout its curriculum, and sustained by Gospel witness" (p. 17).

- Catholic schools transmit Catholic culture through religious symbols and intentionally use physical symbols as representation of identity, as references for teaching, and as a means to help transmit Catholic values (Furst & Denig, 2005).

- Communal organization and an inspirational ideology grounded in shared values of caring and social justice are key areas contributing to the functioning of effective Catholic high schools (Bryk, Lee, & Holland, 1993).

- Teachers' awareness of their own spirituality and ability to express this spirituality favorably impacts the teacher-student relationship and supports the child's spirituality (Kennedy & Duncan, 2006).

- A majority of surveyed Catholic school faculty members note they believe that praying together as a school faculty greatly strengthens the school's Catholic identity, incarnates the school's mission statement, and gives witness to the greater school community (Mayotte, 2010).

- Attendance at Catholic high schools has been shown to have a positive impact on civic responsibilities (Dee, 2005).

CREATING A CATHOLIC CULTURE OF LEARNING

The following areas highlight ways in which the classroom teacher can share in the responsibility of creating a school climate "illumined by the light of faith" (CCE, 1988, §25).

Message

Choosing to foster a Christ-like atmosphere in the classroom, serving as a moral educator, and organizing the classroom space to highlight Catholic identity are concrete ways that teachers can respond to the call to be "witnesses to the faith in both their words and actions" (USCCB, 2005, p. 10).

Fostering a Christ-like atmosphere within the classroom. In a Catholic school classroom, abstract notions of faith can become real to students as they experience Christian values revealed through daily interactions. Showing a sincere interest in each individual student and promoting the respect of all are essential characteristics for creating this Christ-like atmosphere. Moreover, these essential values provide a framework to establish a system for classroom management.

Examples in Action

- Showing care for students expressed in all forms of communication (informal interactions, feedback on work, approaches to instruction, etc.) and through the creation of well-planned and crafted lessons.

- Emphasizing community in the classroom; using a scripture passage like Romans 12:4-6 or 1 Corinthians 12:14-20 to develop a theme of sharing and support of one another.

- Taking advantage of morning meetings in elementary classrooms and homeroom or advisory periods in middle school and high school classrooms to engage students in discussions about issues, struggles, and/or concerns.

- Including ways for students to share about their culture and opportunities to celebrate diversity (a special prayer service, topical discussion to highlight culturally significant feast days and holidays).

Serving as a moral role model. All communication reveals to students qualities of character. Choices of language, content, and expression and coherence of actions and behavior can reveal to students the person of integrity and faith. The teacher whose life expresses this authenticity will have a positive influence on students and likely will help students develop in moral character.

Christ's interactions with the individuals he encountered models how to relate with others. Through prayer and reflection on scripture, a teacher can seek meaningful inspiration for living and revealing virtuous actions.

"During childhood and adolescence a student needs to experience personal relations with outstanding educators, and what is taught has greater influence on the student's formation when placed in a context of personal involvement, genuine reciprocity, coherence of attitudes, lifestyles and day-to-day behavior" (CCE, 1997, §18).

Examples in Action

- Upholding Church teaching in word and action.

- Cultivating an appreciation for truth, honesty, and integrity by modeling a virtuous life and by encouraging concrete expressions by students (through honor codes, etc.).

- Using moral dilemmas (WWJD: What would Jesus do in a given situation?) to engage students in discussions.

- Discussing world events and current issues in light of Gospel values.

Organizing classroom space for highlighting Catholic identity. In a Catholic school classroom, symbols of faith are readily displayed, acknowledged, and referenced. Physical symbols provide a daily reminder of the religious mission of the school; any visitor should notice visible signs that the classroom is a Catholic classroom.

Examples in Action

- Preparing a prayer corner or bulletin board emphasizing aspects of Catholic identity.

- Using visual displays around the classroom: symbols, posters, quotes from scripture, inspirational quotes, sayings of saints, a picture of the pope, a statue or picture of Mary, a Bible.

- Providing a means for students to write intentions (a notebook left in the prayer corner or a slotted box for inserting individual slips of paper on which intentions are written).

Community

In the Catholic school setting, community exists on multiple levels—the classroom, the school, perhaps a local parish, the civic community to which they belong—and interactions occur with varied groups—students, parents, colleagues, school administrators, benefactors, perhaps local parishioners. A teacher can contribute to building up the Christian community through positive words and actions, and presence and participation at events.

Building up the Christian community through positive words and actions. Concrete expressions of support and encouragement are revealed through attentive presence, sympathetic understanding, and generous availability shared within all settings and with all constituents.

> *"The more the members of the educational community develop a real willingness to collaborate among themselves, the more fruitful their work will be. Achieving the educational aims of the school should be an equal priority for teachers, students and families alike, each one according to his or her the Gospel spirit of freedom and love"* (CCE, 1988, §39).

Examples in Action

- Speaking positively about students in every occasion.

- Using discretion when addressing sensitive and/or confidential matters.

- Resolving matters of student conflict peacefully, perhaps through classroom meetings.

- Utilizing the time during advisory periods to build classroom community and involving students in decision making when appropriate.

Supporting the community through presence and participation at events. A visible presence at church and/or school-sponsored events provides witness and notes interest and desire to be an active and involved community member.

Service

Service is an integral aspect of the Gospel message that needs attention in the Catholic classroom. Awareness and action can be encouraged by exposing students to local and world needs and integrating service learning opportunities into the curriculum. A curriculum "imbued with a Catholic worldview" (Miller, 2006) helps to prepare students for service to society and the Church.

Exposing students to local and world needs. The entire curriculum provides opportunity for integrating Gospel values and exposing students to local and world needs.

Integrating age-appropriate service learning opportunities into the curriculum. Attention to service learning needs to occur at all grade levels in developmentally appropriate ways. Needs that are recognized as meaningful by the students are likely to generate greater interest and responsibility to bring about determined goals.

Examples in Action

- Involving students in choice of service projects. At the elementary level, this might include collections for local needs or cards to senior citizens. At the middle school level, ideas might include a buddy system, elderly adoption program or inter-grade program. High school ideas might include peer mediation groups, letters to congressmen concerning current issues, or a fundraising activity to send money to a third world country.

- Encouraging service to parish or civic activities.

"The vocation of every Catholic [Christian] educator includes the work of ongoing social development: to form men and women who will be ready to take their place in society, preparing them in such a way that they will make the kind of social commitment which will enable them to work for the improvement of social structures, making these structures more conformed to the principles of the Gospel. Thus, they will form human beings who will make human society more peaceful, fraternal, and communitarian" (SCCE, 1982, §19).

Thanksgiving and Worship

When Pope Benedict XVI visited the United States in 2008, he addressed Catholic educators and noted to them "that each and every aspect of your learning communities reverberate within the ecclesial life of faith" (p. 3). As noted previously, faith must be communicated within instruction and revealed through interactions. It also must be nurtured in the school community through prayer and the celebration of the sacraments. A classroom teacher has the privilege of praying with the students and working with them to prepare and celebrate special liturgical events.

Praying with students. This obvious point can't be emphasized enough. A prayer to begin a lesson, the school day, or afternoon session can help students focus on what is most essential.

"Catholic education is above all a question of communicating Christ, of helping to form Christ in the lives of others. In the expression of the Second Vatican Council, those who have been baptized must be made ever more aware of the gift of faith that they have received, they must learn to adore the Father in spirit and in truth, and they must be trained to live the newness of Christian life in justice and in the holiness of truth" (John Paul II, 1979).

Examples in Action

- Offering a simple invocation to begin a lesson: "Holy Spirit, enlighten us. Most Sacred Heart of Jesus, we place our trust in you. Saint (school patron), pray for us."

- Encouraging students to lead the prayer (using a calendar template and assigning students a day to lead prayer or asking for a volunteer daily).

- Teaching students common prayers of the Catholic Church and the parts and responses of the Mass.

- Actively participating in school liturgies as a lector, cantor, or Eucharistic minister, giving witness to students.

Preparing a variety of prayer experiences with students. Students can be involved in the planning and facilitation of prayer services and in the planning of school or class liturgies.

Examples in Action

- Inviting students to assume roles in the Mass (lector, choir member, acolyte, etc.).

- Utilizing the liturgical year calendar and highlighting significant feasts and saints of the Church (see Figure 1 and Table 1).

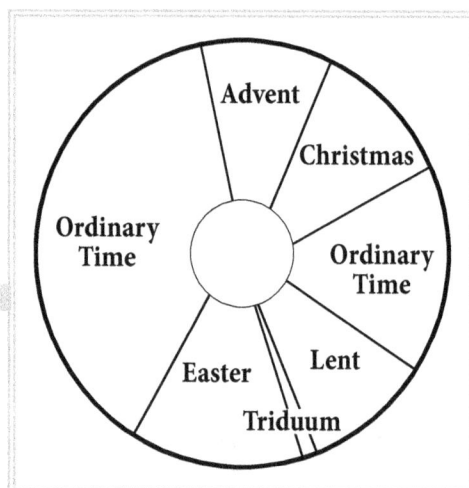

Figure 1. Liturgical Calendar

Table 1. *Liturgical Year*

Month*	Liturgical Season and Color	Significant Highlights	Ideas for the Classroom Elementary Middle school High school
August/ September	Ordinary Time GREEN		• Write a class prayer. (E) • Discuss the life and mission of the patron saint/namesake of the school. (E, M, or H)
October	Ordinary Time GREEN	• Month of the Holy Rosary • *October 4*: Memorial of St. Francis of Assisi	• Pray a daily decade of the rosary. (E, M, or H) • Offer a simple invocation to Mary: "Queen of the Holy Rosary, pray for us." (E, M, or H) • Create a prayer service for the blessing of animals on the Memorial of St. Francis of Assisi. (E)
November	Ordinary Time GREEN	• *November 1*: All Saints Day • *November 2*: All Souls Day • *Thanksgiving*	• Use a simple journal to create a book of remembrance and place in your prayer corner. Include remembrance of the deceased throughout the month during daily prayer. (M or H) • Highlight cultural traditions associated with Día de los Muertos, the Day of the Dead. (E, M, or H) • Use a simple journal to create a book of gratitude and place in your prayer corner. Read one or two of the entries during daily prayer throughout the month. (E or M)
December	Advent PURPLE	• *December 6*: Memorial of St. Nicholas • *December 8*: Solemnity of the Immaculate Conception • *December 12*: Feast of Our Lady of Guadalupe	• Involve students in preparing Advent prayer services. (M or H) • Celebrate the Memorial of St. Nicholas with older students providing special treats for younger students. (M)

* Months of the year associated with liturgical seasons are approximated time spans.

Table 1. *Liturgical Year* (continued)

Month*	Liturgical Season and Color	Significant Highlights	Ideas for the Classroom Elementary **Middle school** **High school**
January	Christmas WHITE	• *Last week of January*: Catholic Schools Week	• Incorporate the Catholic Schools Week theme in activities throughout the week. (E, M, or H)
February	Ordinary Time GREEN Lent PURPLE	• Beginning of Lent	• Encourage prayer and concrete actions of service during the season of Lent in order to make it a more meaningful season. (E, M, or H)
March	Lent PURPLE	• *March 17*: Feast of St. Patrick • *March 19*: Feast of St. Joseph	• Consider involving middle school students in a dramatization of the Stations of the Cross. (M) • Involve students in creating a Stations of the Cross prayer booklet with drawings and composed prayers. (E or M) • Visit the school chapel for a special prayer service. (H)
	Triduum		
April	Easter Season WHITE		• Have students look for signs of new life during a nature walk. Make connections to Easter season. (E)
May	Ordinary Time GREEN	• The month of Mary	• Consider involving elementary children in a May crowning ritual or living rosary. (E)
June	Ordinary Time GREEN		• Share a prayer to bring closure to the school year. (E, M, or H)

* Months of the year associated with liturgical seasons are approximated time spans.

High School Teaching

A Catholic Classroom, more than anything you "put" in it or even any thing you "do" in it, is made by the person and the teacher you "are" in it. A Catholic teacher makes a Catholic classroom. How you make this idea a reality should be the focus of your professional and spiritual work. To offer some rough guidelines. . . . a healthy and developed prayer life is essential for teaching students how to pray well. Actively engaging in service beyond and outside of the classroom is essential for modeling a life of service (you are busy, but it could be as little as an hour a week). Participating in the Eucharist, perhaps even more than once a week, will enrich your understanding and appreciation for the "source and summit" of the Catholic Faith. Reading and reflecting upon Scripture, the primary source of revelation in the Christian tradition, is fundamental to being able to teach the Christian tradition well.

— Anthony D'Agostino

Symbols of our faith serve as important reminders and having a quiet corner or an open Bible to the day's readings is a good idea. These are especially effective if you use them and refer to them from time to time. This way they don't just become nice decorations. The most important part of a Catholic classroom is the environment you create—accepting, nurturing, loving, patient, and safe. Students adopt an attitude of acceptance and belonging, which they take with them long after they leave your classroom, and which will have a more lasting impact than the nice decorations we put on our walls.

— Matt Reichert

It is important for your students to know that you practice what you preach. When you ask them for special intentions at prayer time, make sure you add your own. They are truly paying attention.

— Noah Beacom

I displayed biblical quotes in my high school classroom, as well as quotes by Mother Teresa. In my French classes, we had a special lesson on the feast day of Our Lady of Lourdes. During it we listened to the rosary in French (participated in the prayers the students had learned) and learned about the feast day.

— Michelle Blair

Middle School Teaching

Involve religion whenever possible. This can be as simple as praying at the beginning of the day and before each class begins. If you teach religion, you can even do regular activities such as praying the Rosary as a class once a month. Another great idea is working religion into different subjects (which will involve co-planning with other teachers if you are in middle or high school). For example, your class can discuss the Church's views on evolution when students learn about this in science. To do this, you need to be aware of what students are learning in their other classes, and then capitalize on the cross-curricular moments.

— Brett Guy

After graduating, I am working at a charter school. I miss working in a Catholic school for many reasons, but I think I miss beginning class with prayer the most. It's a simple, yet wonderful way to remind students (and teachers) that they have a constant source of support, love, and forgiveness. The classroom is a place of success and cooperation as well as mistakes and sometimes competition. In the midst of all that takes place, a moment of quiet time to refocus one's purpose is essential.

— *Laura Farrell*

I wanted my students to learn the importance of saying thank you to those who helped our class. During homeroom, we would discuss people we needed to thank. I asked one student to make a thank you letter for the class, and every student would sign it.

— *Anna Arias*

Begin every class with a reflection and a prayer. Another wonderful idea to incorporate into your class is a "Prayer Partner." Choose friends of yours who may need your prayers, or people who have interesting jobs, wonderful stories, and unique ways of praying. Each week choose a new prayer partner and have your students write him or her a letter of how they will pray for him or her. Meanwhile, have your prayer partner send your class a letter and post card about himself or herself and answer the student's questions about who they are, how they pray, and how they will pray for your class. Chart the people by posting their post cards around a map of the United States or world.

— *Lauren Flynn*

In January the eighth grade class led the school's "Souper Bowl" drive. This is an event in which the eighth graders went class to class to speak to students about the problem of homelessness and the need to raise money for local soup kitchens. The Souper Bowl was presented as a time to think about those who do not have a home in which to enjoy the football game nor the food and beverages that we usually associate with the Super Bowl. Students went from class to class collecting spare change and donations. They donated the money to the Iron Gate, a local soup kitchen at which they had previously volunteered. This fundraiser was especially meaningful because students had direct experience with the people and place that would benefit from the money they raised.

— *Meghan Finerghty*

When I was teaching in Birmingham—and even as a teacher now in Chicago—I had a lot of students who were not Catholic, but I had to somehow create a Catholic environment for learning even though most students were not Catholic. Respect and recognizing God in others is an essential goal of the Catholic classroom. One thing I always have had students do at the beginning of the year (and again later when they begin to forget) is to write one good thing they see in each student in the class. What do they respect or how do they see God in their classmates? Then I create an individualized list for each student so that they can see what their classmates think of them. Students often decorate them and hang them on the front of their desks, and I frequently refer and point to them throughout the year.

— *Katie Key*

Elementary School Teaching

Make sure you lay out your religion corner in such a way that invites the students to visit it. Include a chair and loads of cushions so the children can write, read, pray, or reflect. Leave plenty of Bible stories and readable material (with pictures) for them, a Rosary (with guidelines of how to pray it), etc. I had a prayer box where the children wrote a prayer or a worry they might have had and this was kept between God and me. Many students are afraid to say aloud how they are thinking or feeling. This was a great way for the students to get close to God and not feel alone in their worries/concerns. Nobody else reads the notes/prayers and they are addressed "Dear God/Lord." I found out many disturbing things about my students and was able to respond to calls of help. Also in a positive way it was great for the children to pray for their relatives and friends without having to say it aloud.

— *Heather Barker*

The foundation of my efforts to develop spirituality in my classroom stems from Community Circle every morning. Nearly every day we have a quick morning meeting in which every student is able to share something they brought or events happening in their lives. I learn a lot about the students from this, and I like to share things going on in my life with them as well. I believe this provides the students with an environment in which they become more and more comfortable and open with each other. We then say an opening prayer from our prayer book that I made for the class, have special intentions, and say a closing prayer. Each week a different student is prayer leader and chooses the opening and closing prayers. During the intentions the students can pray for whatever they would like as long as it is respectful to God.   — *Nick Dailey*

Another teacher showed me an idea for a student-focused "Christ Shines Through" bulletin board. I really liked the idea because it suggests that students are all different, unique and special in the eyes of God. It teaches students that Christ is in everyone, just in different ways. I have students complete four categories: family, hobbies, favorite television show/movie, and favorite book. They also must name words and actions they say and do that show they are a child of God. Once the student has completed these pages, their bulletin board gets to stay up for two weeks. This is not only a good way to incorporate religion into everyday life, but it allows students to take ownership of their classroom and its decor. The students also are very encouraging to each other about their displays.   — *Katie Cawley*

My classroom ran by the "Golden Rule," which is of course that we treat others as we ourselves would like to be treated. We spent a lot of time at the start of the school year examining the Biblical foundations of this rule and discussing ways we should use this notion to govern how we treat others in the classroom. I bought my students each a small wooden cross to wear every day at school. These were simple, but they really helped the students to see themselves as a Catholic community in my classroom. The crosses were only worn at school; they took them off and hung them on their coat hooks at the end of the day. We also talked about how by wearing these crosses, we were keeping Jesus close to our hearts.   — *Amy Bozzo*

It can be fun to link your classroom management rewards with elements of the Catholic classroom. For instance, students can work towards earning a Rosary-making party. After a week of good behavior, a Friday afternoon can be devoted to making rosaries with multi-colored beads and yarn. Students enjoy picking out the sequences of colors and learning about which prayers are associated with which beads.   — *Lindsay Fitzpatrick*

My students really enjoyed learning how to pray the Rosary. I was able to get some of those plastic rosaries for the classroom so each student had one to use. We would go to our reading circle (which became the prayer circle) and students would take turns leading a decade (or more). Before or after we would pray, we would learn about one of the mysteries. It was just neat to see them appreciate that prayer time.…Every morning, we began with journal, but the topics changed each day. One day a week, we did morality questions. The students were given a scenario and asked how they would respond and why. They would discuss their responses as a class. It was really effective because they learned from one another and as the year progressed their responses were more informed and you could see the development of their consciences.…They loved moral discussion journal day.
                                                                                                       — *Brynn Johnson*

Always have a place where the students can go and write their own prayers. It is a humbling experience when a ten-year-old can teach you how to pray and be thankful for all of God's little gifts in our lives.

— *Patrick Vogtner*

In my prayer corner, I have a sign which says "Let Us Pray" and a stack of crosses made out of construction paper. Children may write their special intentions on these crosses at any time. As a class, we often pray for the intentions on these crosses and in our hearts. — *Courtney Jianas Vogtner*

During Lent my students created a bulletin board display that we titled, "Blossoming from Darkness to Light." At the beginning of Lent we put up a stem and the center of a flower. Every time a student acted in a way that demonstrated prayerfulness, abstinence, or fasting they wrote their name and the action on a flower petal. Each week the flower petal changed to a lighter shade. — *Clare Murphy*

The Respectful Teacher

I pray, loving God,
that you keep me mindful
of my responsibility and desire
to share through my teaching
the utmost respect in word, in action,
in thought, and in prayer.

    With Jesus as my model,
    may I choose humble actions,
    gentle listening, wise words,
    and an honoring presence.

        If I am less than respectful,
        I pray for forgiveness.
        If I am curt or arrogant,
        I pray for awareness.
        If I am preoccupied or distant,
        I pray for attention.

Loving God,
Help me to treat each person
with the same level of respect.
Help me to reveal to my students
that I value their presence and their being.
Shape my words and actions
to reveal your gentle kindness.
Mark my teaching with humility
and reverence for others.

    Through these actions may others know
    the sincerity of encouraging phrases,
    trusting looks, and valued presence.

    For this I pray. Amen.

REFERENCES

Benedict XVI. (2008, April). *Meeting with Catholic educators.* Vatican City: Libreria Editrice Vaticana. Retrieved July 28, 2009, from http://www.vatican.va/holy_father/benedict_xvi/speeches/2008/april/documents/hf_ben-xvi_spe_20080417_cath-univ-washington_en.html

Bryk, A. S., Lee, V. E., & Holland, P. B. (1993). *Catholic schools and the common good.* Cambridge, MA: Harvard University Press.

Congregation for Catholic Education. (1997). *The Catholic school on the threshold of the third millennium.* Rome: Libreria Editrice Vaticana.

Congregation for Catholic Education. (1988). *The religious dimension of education in a Catholic school.* Washington, DC: United States Catholic Conference.

Dee, T. (2005). The effects of Catholic schooling on civic participation. *International Tax and Public Finance, 12*, 605-625.

Furst, L., & Denig, S. (2005). The use of physical symbols to transmit culture in religious schools: A comparison of Adventist and Catholic schools in America. *Journal of Empirical Theology, 18*(1), 1-21.

John Paul II. (1979). *Message to the National Catholic Educational Association of the United States, April 16, 1979.* Retrieved March 17, 2010, from http://www.vatican.va/holy_father/john_paul_ii/speeches/1979/april/documents/hf_jp-ii_spe_19790416_usa-scuola-catt_en.html

Kennedy, A., & Duncan, J. (2006). New Zealand children's spirituality in Catholic schools: Teachers' perspectives. *International Journal of Children's Spirituality, 11*(2), 281-292.

Mayotte, G. (2010). Faculty prayer in Catholic schools: A survey of practices and meaning. *Catholic Education: A Journal of Inquiry and Practice, 13*(3), 329-349.

Mayotte, G. (2007). *Prayers to guide teaching.* Notre Dame, IN: Alliance for Catholic Education Press.

Miller, J. M. (2006). *The Holy See's teaching on Catholic schools.* Atlanta, GA: Solidarity Association.

Sacred Congregation for Catholic Education. (1982). *Lay Catholics in schools: Witnesses to faith.* Washington, DC: United States Catholic Conference.

United States Conference of Catholic Bishops. (2005). *Renewing our commitment to Catholic elementary and secondary schools in the third millennium.* Washington, DC: Author.

Reflect upon the fourfold purpose of Christian education outlined by the United States bishops noted on page 3. How do you envision message, community, service, and thanksgiving being expressed in your classroom? Take time to write concrete expressions for each of these categories.

Message
(Beyond instruction in Catholic doctrine)

1. Fostering a Christ-like atmosphere within the classroom
2. Serving as a moral role model
3. Organizing the classroom space for highlighting Catholic identity

Community

1. Building up the Christian community through positive words and actions
2. Supporting the community through presence and participation in events

Service

1. Exposing students to local and world needs
2. Integrating age-appropriate service learning opportunities into the curriculum

Thanksgiving and Worship

1. Praying with students
2. Preparing a variety of prayer experiences with students

Procedures and Routines

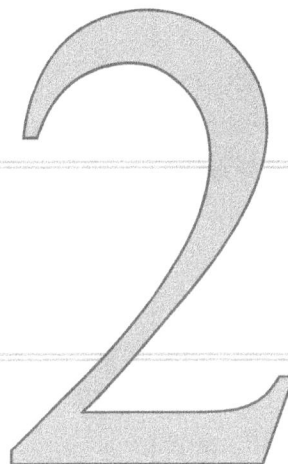

Procedures outline a teacher's expectations for how common classroom practices should occur. They become routines when they have been learned thoroughly and students undertake them automatically.

Many aspects of classroom life benefit from having practical and efficient procedures and these include a variety of instructional, organizational, and/or functional tasks. Because the classroom is a community, emphasis on shared responsibility for care of the common space and respect for the individuals utilizing it are important areas to highlight when reinforcing procedures.

Preparation and practice are the keys to successful implementation of procedures. Prior to the start of the school year, a teacher should plan out expectations for all anticipated needs. Then, during the first few days of school and as a specific need arises, the procedure related to the need must be taught and sufficiently practiced. According to McEwan (2006) it is important that procedures become routine during the first 3 weeks of school in order that they be utilized effectively during the remaining 33 weeks. For this reason it remains absolutely essential that procedures be introduced, taught, modeled, practiced, and reinforced during the first few weeks of the year.

The topic of procedures generally falls under the category of classroom management, a term that readily describes both rules and procedures. Though rules will be the topic of the next section, they generally work hand in hand with the implementation of effective procedures in securing a quality learning environment.

WHAT RESEARCH SAYS

- Teachers who are good classroom managers utilize explicit techniques to manage the learning environment (Marzano, 2003). Giving attention to classroom management at the start of the school year is essential for a productive classroom.

- The number of disruptions in classrooms where rules and procedures are effectively implemented are significantly lower than the amount of disruptions in classrooms where they are not effectively implemented (Marzano, 2003). This is true at all grade levels.

CONSIDERATIONS WHEN PLANNING PROCEDURES

Efficient classroom environments do not occur automatically nor will students automatically know what is expected of them. A teacher needs to provide clear directions to make procedures known and lots of practice to help procedures become routine. This is true at all grade levels.

When setting up procedures lots of factors need to be considered. First, be sure to reference the school handbook or talk to your school principal, an assigned mentor, or veteran colleague. Some routines might already be established and utilized by the entire school community. Contradicting such routines will only confuse students and might not even be allowed. Second, be sure to establish age appropriate procedures. A repetition clapping procedure to call for student attention is likely to elicit laughter in a high school classroom while use of the same approach in a second grade classroom is likely to focus student attention very effectively. Third, aim for efficiency when setting up procedures so that little instructional time is lost when doing housekeeping or administrative tasks. The purpose of having good routines is that more time can be devoted to learning. Finally, keep procedures simple. Students are far more likely to recall simple procedures than complicated approaches.

Consider introducing procedures as needed. You might introduce the expectations for classroom arrival and dismissal on the first day of school as these procedures need to be utilized immediately. You might only introduce the expectation for paper headings the first time an assignment is to be prepared by the students. Once a procedure is introduced and in order to help it become routine, be consistent with expectations for use thereafter.

Listed below are areas for consideration when developing procedures, questions to guide the process, helpful practices in action, and ideas taken from sample management plans. (Note the following codes: E=elementary, M=middle school, H=high school.)

Beginning the School Day/Class Period

When students arrive to your classroom, will there be posted work awaiting them? If so, what will it be? How will you handle tasks like documenting attendance and tardiness or taking lunch counts? How will you greet students, share announcements, and facilitate prayer?

Areas to consider:

- Use of morning work (E) or bell work (M, H)
- Administrative tasks—attendance, lunch tallies, tardiness (E, M); attendance, tardiness (H)
- Prayer
- Pledge of Allegiance (said at all levels once during the school day)
- Morning calendar (early E)
- Announcements—birthdays, special social events, intercom, etc.
- Practices for review or collection of homework and for obtaining missing work from previously absent students

Examples in Action

- Having work posted for students upon their arrival to the classroom (daily language or math activity, journal prompt, appropriate bell work question for lesson under study). Have students get into the routine of beginning the work immediately and working quietly. This is a valuable and productive use of time that allows for administrative tasks (taking attendance, collecting lunch money, obtaining missing work from previously absent students, reviewing or collecting homework) to occur efficiently.

- Creating an efficient system for documenting attendance. In elementary grades, this might involve students moving a clothespin, magnet, or craft stick with their name on it to an "IN" column to note their presence. In the middle grades, students might rotate recording the class attendance as an assigned classroom job. In high school classrooms, a teacher might simply canvas the room while students complete their bell work.

- Having students place homework on their desks while working on bell work; walking around to check homework for "neat, complete, and organized" and recording it as such on a grade sheet.

- Creating a class bulletin board to post a birthday calendar, school notices, and other significant events. This information can be referenced during announcements.

- Holding morning meetings as part of a daily routine in elementary classrooms; inviting student sharing of significant happenings in their lives during them.

Sample Management Plan Statements*
Attendance and Prayer Procedures

HIGH SCHOOL TEACHER

Prayer
Prayer will begin after the bell rings. Prayer will signal the beginning of class. It will start by making the Sign of the Cross. Some days I will lead prayer, other days students will lead prayer.

Taking Attendance
Attendance will be taken after prayer. Students who are late must go to the office for a pass to class, which is recorded by the office.

MIDDLE SCHOOL TEACHER

Attendance
Attendance will be recorded while students work independently on their board assignment.

Prayer
Morning devotion will come over the intercom. Students will be doing morning work until devotion. When devotion begins, students will rise and participate in morning devotion which includes prayers, psalms, the pledge to the flag, and the school creed. In later classes, prayer will begin each class. Prayer will be led by the teacher, with a voluntary option to students as the year progresses.

ELEMENTARY SCHOOL TEACHER

Attendance, Notes, etc. (Grade 2)
As students complete morning work, I complete the attendance sheet. I walk around to each student's desk to collect notes, homework, etc.

Morning Calendar, Announcements, Prayer, Pledge of Allegiance (Grade 2)
Students stand at the sound of the bell for the school opening prayer and for the Pledge of Allegiance, led by our principal. Following the pledge, we will discuss the day of the week, write the date on our board and review our days and months. Our class will sing our good morning song and then one student will come forward to lead the class in a review of the class rules. Finally we will discuss the value of the month and one way to model it throughout our day.

*Sample management plan statements throughout this chapter provided by Allison Astuno, Kathleen Burke, Patrick Kaiser, Michael O'Connor, Sarah Runger, and Brendan Ryan.

Transitions and Interruptions

What will be your expectations regarding how students enter the classroom and move through the hallways? How will you dismiss students? How will you handle requests for bathroom use, a drink of water, or pencil sharpening? What are the school requirements regarding emergency drills?

Areas to consider:

- Movement to and from the classroom
- Entering and exiting the classroom
- Dismissal at the end of a class period (H, possibly M)
- Bathroom use and/or use of the drinking fountain
- Use of the pencil sharpener (E, M, possibly H)
- Use of the cafeteria
- Use of the playground (E)
- Fire and disaster drills

Examples in Action

- Checking with school administration about procedures for fire and disaster drills.

- Monitoring students at all times. If some students are standing in the hallway and others in the classroom, stand at the classroom door to have an eye on both groups.

- Limiting the amount of movement by students so they can more readily focus on engaging in the lesson.

Sample Management Plan Statements
Procedures for Entering and Exiting the Classroom,
Sharpening Pencils, and Bathroom Use

HIGH SCHOOL TEACHER

Entering the Classroom
When students enter the classroom, they will be expected to sit down and talk quietly among themselves until class begins. They should have their homework ready to be collected.

Dismissing the Class
Class will be dismissed verbally after the bell has sounded.

Pencil Sharpening
This must be done before or after class. If a pencil breaks, the student is allowed to sharpen it when it is not distracting to the class. If a student does not have a pencil, I will sell one for 25 cents.

Bathroom Use
Students must ask permission to leave their seats, and are only allowed to leave the classroom for an approved reason. Only one student at a time will be permitted to leave. That student must take my hall pass. I am responsible for student safety. Students cannot learn if they are not in the classroom. Approved reasons for leaving do not include routine bathroom breaks.

MIDDLE SCHOOL TEACHER

Entering the Classroom
When students arrive in the classroom, they are first to look at the board to see what is required for class that day. Next, students will go to their lockers (located in the classroom). Students will take out what they need for class and leave everything else (including their backpacks) in their lockers. Students will move to their desks quietly and orderly. Name cards on the desks will designate where students will sit (in alphabetical order). Students will sit and begin morning work on the board.

Leaving the Classroom (at the end of class or at any other time)
When class ends, students will wait for the teacher's instructions. The teacher will ask the students to rise and line up on the side of the room where the lockers are located. Students will dispose of any trash from their desks in the wastebasket as they are filing out. The teacher will collect the cards or other assignments at the door as the students are leaving, being certain to observe activity both inside the classroom and in the hallway.

Pencil Sharpening
Pencils should be sharpened before class begins; the pencil sharpener may not be used during class.

Signing Out of the Classroom
If a student receives the acknowledging nod to leave the classroom, the student will then walk to the check-out board. On this clipboard, the student will write down his or her name, destination

(most commonly bathroom or water fountain), and time of departure. The student will then take the appropriate pass. When the student returns, he or she will return the pass to the table and mark his or her time of arrival. The student will then return to his or her seat in silence. *Additional notes:* One pass exists for leaving the classroom. This is to be used for emergency visits to the office, bathrooms, water fountain, and other classrooms. Only one person is allowed out of the classroom at any given time.

ELEMENTARY SCHOOL TEACHER

Entering the Classroom (Grade 2)

Upon arrival at the door, students will cross the "quiet line" (a line of tape placed in the doorway on the floor). Once the students cross the line, they must be silent as they unpack and settle in to their morning work. Students will immediately empty the contents of their backpack onto their desk, hang up their coats and backpacks, then return to their desk and put everything away. A timer will be set as soon as the last student crosses "the quiet line" (initially the timer will be set for 5 minutes but this will be altered after observing how it works for the class). Once the timer sounds, all students should be seated with everything put away, and working on their board work.

Exiting the Classroom (Grade 5)

Before we leave the classroom, the line must be straight and students must not be talking. A sign will hang above the door reminding students of these line rules.

Pencil Sharpening

Grade 2: All students are expected to remain in their seats throughout independent work. If their pencil breaks, they are to raise their hand and I will bring them a new, freshly-sharpened one.

Grade 5: There will be a number of sharpened pencils for students to use. If they break a pencil they can walk to the side of the room where the pencils are located and place the broken one in the broken box and pick up a sharpened one. Students will be allowed to get up to get a new pencil if they can do so quietly. However, students are to have more than one sharpened pencil in their desk at the beginning of each day to minimize the number of times students need to get a new pencil. This policy will be implemented the first day.

Bathroom Use

Grade 2: Our class has an established bathroom break during the mid-morning and again during the lunch/recess period (or immediately after). Aside from these times, students are discouraged from using the restroom or water fountain because no one wants to miss out on the fun and learning in the classroom! Of course, sometimes students will need to use the restroom outside of these times, in which case there is a bathroom pass.

Grade 5: Students will be allowed to use the bathroom during work time but not during lessons, unless it is an emergency. I will have a pass they are to carry with them. Only one student will be allowed to leave for the bathroom at a time. I will remind students to use the bathroom during any breaks in the day.

During Lessons

How do you plan to get student attention, distribute or collect materials, collect and/or review homework, and have students respond to questions (raising hands or calling out answers)? How will students be expected to prepare paper headings or signal a need for help? Will students be allowed to move around the room to sharpen a pencil, get a tissue, or throw away a paper? If so, what parameters will you set for such movement?

Areas to consider:

- Getting student attention
- Student participation
- Homework review/collection
- Distributing and collecting materials
- Paper headings
- When a student needs help
- Out-of-seat procedures
- What to do when work is completed
- Test procedures

Examples in Action

- Encouraging students to raise hands to signal a desire to participate or a need for a tissue, sharpened pencil, or help with independent work. Allowing students to call out responses may be chaotic and is much more difficult to manage. It also inhibits quieter students from responding.

- Posting a list of ideas/expectations for what to do when work is completed (i.e., read a book, work on folder activity, etc.).

Sample Management Plan Statements
Procedures for Getting Student Attention and Paper Headings

HIGH SCHOOL TEACHER

Paper Headings

Each student will head papers with his or her name, the date, class period, and the assignment. This will be located in the top left corner of the paper. Each extra page is expected to be headed in a similar way. I will have this procedure demonstrated on a poster in my classroom.

MIDDLE SCHOOL TEACHER

Getting Student Attention

When the teacher wishes to have the students' attention, he will raise his hand in silence. When students see the teacher's hand, they will raise their hands. As they raise their hands, they will stop moving and talking, giving full attention to the teacher. If the students are too noisy, the teacher will count down aloud and with his fingers, either from 5 or 3 to 1. When the teacher reaches 1, the students should be quiet and ready.

Paper Headings

The first line of the heading will include the student's name. The second line will be for the grade and the subject. The third line will have the assignment. The date will be on the fourth line.

ELEMENTARY SCHOOL TEACHER

Getting Student Attention

Grade 2: "Quiet Coyote." Ears open, mouths closed. I put up the quiet coyote and begin counting down from 5 and students are expected to face front, close their mouths, and put up their own coyote, ready to begin the next lesson.

Grade 5: When I want the students' attention, I will quietly stand at the front of the class and raise my hand. I will tell them on the first day that when they see my hand raised they are to sit down, be quiet, and raise their hand as well. I will tell them that class will not continue until everyone is quiet and their hands are raised. I will practice this multiple times on the first day by having them do short discussion activities, or "partner share," and then raise my hand to get them to stop.

Preparing Papers for Assignment

Any piece of work should have the student's name at the top of the paper. If the work is something other than a worksheet, the paper should have a heading which follows the established procedure (name, date, subject, assignment or page #).

Ending the School Day

How will students prepare for school dismissal? What responsibilities for care of the classroom will they share?

Areas to consider:
- Packing up materials
- Housekeeping routines
- Distributing school notices
- Prayer

Examples in Action

- Assigning students classroom jobs to share in the care of the classroom.

- Utilizing any leftover minutes to engage students with a review of math facts, spelling words, or a sharing of weekend happenings. The few final minutes can be a great time for review and/or building rapport.

Sample Management Plan Statements
Procedures for Housekeeping and Packing Up Materials

HIGH SCHOOL TEACHER

Assigning Homework
Homework is written on the board at the end of class. It is clearly stated and expected that students copy the assignment into their assignment notebook. All homework should be done on loose leaf paper.

MIDDLE SCHOOL TEACHER

Dismissal
Students will go to their lockers in groups called by the teacher each afternoon. They will be dismissed by the teacher and will line up at the bottom of the stairs where they will wait for the teacher to direct them outside. Students should not roam the halls after school.

ELEMENTARY SCHOOL TEACHER

Packing Up (Grade 2)
All students will take out assignment books and write down the homework together. As a class, we will take out the books which are necessary to bring home for the night and each student will pile these books on top of the desk. Each student will take out their yellow "[Student Name]'s Important Papers" folder. Any notices which need to go home and remain at home will be distributed and placed in the left pocket (labeled "Mine to Keep") and those which need to be signed and returned to school will be placed in the right pocket (labeled "Sign and Bring Back") and should remain on top of the desk as well. Students will be called individually to get their backpack, pack everything, and return to their seat. Once there, they continue the assigned work while everyone packs. If everyone is finished, I will read a chapter from a novel. Students will then stand for closing prayer when the principal comes on the intercom with announcements. After prayer, I call students by row to line up and go out to the parking lot for the final bell. Once the bell rings, students must hand me their dismissal card so that I know where they are going for the afternoon (after-care, tutoring, home).

Housekeeping (Grade 5)
I will assign students each week to have a role for cleaning up, such as the pencil sharpener, board eraser, and homework organizer. Students will do these jobs in the last few minutes of class along with students cleaning everything off their desks and picking up paper or trash around the room. I will not dismiss the class until all of the housekeeping is complete.

High School Teaching

Develop procedures and good, constructive habits as soon as possible. For example, always collect homework, give assignments, get students' attention, run group work, and give directions in the same or similar way. Then students will eventually automatically respond in the way you want. Also, know the difference between a procedure and a rule. Rules have consequences and govern things that are more serious, such as issues of respect and academic honesty. There are no consequences for not following procedures other than reminders or even practice. Developing strong procedures and habits right away will have a significant effect on your classroom management, your teaching, and your rapport with your students.

— Matt Reichert

Procedures and practice are truly key to a well-run classroom environment. If students feel that their classroom is well-run, they are less likely to spend time goofing off. Strike a balance between being too formal or too loose by both practicing your procedures thoroughly and making fun of yourself for having to be so thorough. Students might appreciate that human touch.

— Noah Beacom

I learned that if you make the exact number of copies of a handout for a class, and there are two leftover, that if you put the two absent students' names on those papers right away and put them in a particular folder for the student for the next day, it can ensure that the student receives the work in a timely manner.

— Annie Walorski Morin

Middle School Teaching

My best strategy for the first week of school, when setting up my rules and procedures, was to practice over and over with note cards. I wrote out about twenty note cards with different situations and comments that I anticipated would happen during the year. Then I shuffled them and handed them out. I called on students one by one to read their card, and then the class would guess how I would handle the situation, and then I would act it out. Of course, we would ham it up and get a little bit silly, but we were also very clear about all possible circumstances for most normal procedures. We did this for discipline issues as well.

— David Yeager

Having multiple ways of getting students attention is imperative. If you only have one way, it will not be as effective later in the year. Some methods include the clap method (clap once if you can hear me, clap twice if you can hear me…), turning the lights off and having everyone "freeze," and the hand raised and mouth not moving method. With procedures, scaffolding and modeling are important ways to ensure student understanding. Do not assume anything; it never hurts to review a procedure and model a behavior.

— Rory Dippold

I found it extremely helpful to have a specific box for assignments for each class. In addition, I have a specific box for the graded assignments for each class so that I can remember to return these during the next class.

— Anna Arias

When I think about my first two years of teaching in regard to procedures and practice, I think of endurance. Sometimes you have to have the students do the same thing over and over again until they get it right. When students were talking while in line, I remember I used to have some of my students line up more than ten times before they got it right. Whatever procedures you put in place, make sure you practice it and demand excellence, even if it takes 100 times to get it.   — *Katie Key*

As a middle school teacher and particularly now as a sixth grade homeroom teacher, I see the importance of helping the students with organization. Now it is often called "executive functioning skills," but this is something students entering middle school for the first time definitely need help with. Even if you need to take five extra minutes at the end of every class period to allow students to write down their homework and put papers away in the correct folders under your supervision, these are all things that will help them become more responsible and organized as they assimilate to middle school.

                                                                                                  — *Katie Key*

Elementary School Teaching

The biggest tip I could offer is to have lots of procedures and to drill your students until those procedures are second nature. Also, make sure you have a strong morning routine. I had my students come in to the room, and they were not allowed to speak until I asked if anyone had any questions. They knew how to use our attendance board, turn in homework, unpack their things, and sit down to work quietly on the journals while I scurried around doing all the "morning stuff" that teachers have to do. The silence in the morning was golden, and all the students got everything done that they needed to do in the morning as well.   — *Amy Bozzo*

Always rehearse stopping points when walking somewhere. Get it to a point where students know where to stop when you're going somewhere.   — *Brynn Johnson*

Even if it's as simple as walking down the hall or lining up in front of the classroom, have the students tell you how it should be done. Do some practice runs; they like showing off how good they can be.

                                                                                              — *Patrick Vogtner*

One fun idea is to have a "Mystery Walker" when walking in the halls. If the mystery walker is walking in the manner described by the teacher (quietly, arms by his or her side, etc.), the class will earn a point. The teacher announces the mystery walker if the child earns the class a point. However, the teacher does not announce the child if he or she does not earn the class a point.

                                                                                       — *Courtney Jianas Vogtner*

As with most second grade classrooms, each year I often have problems with tattling. I try to use certain vocabulary with the students to help the problem. Tattling is telling me something because you are trying to get someone else in trouble. Telling is when you are giving me important information that I need to know to keep our classroom a better place. Often when a child approaches me (especially after recess) I ask them, "Are you telling me something important that I need to know or are you tattling?"

                                                                                              — *Clare Murphy*

Creating procedures is not just for the students. Procedures will make your life so much easier. With practice, most students will pick up on how you want things done. Then you can focus on the few students who struggle to follow directions.   — *Maggie Schroeder*

REFERENCES

Marzano, R. (2003). *Classroom management that works: Research-based strategies for every teacher.* Alexandria, VA: Association for Supervision and Curriculum Development.

McEwan, E. (2006). *How to survive and thrive in the first three weeks of school.* Thousand Oaks, CA: Corwin Press.

TEMPLATES

Here are some seating arrangement ideas for starting the school year. Think about what would work best for you to engage students in learning. Which would be easiest for you to manage?

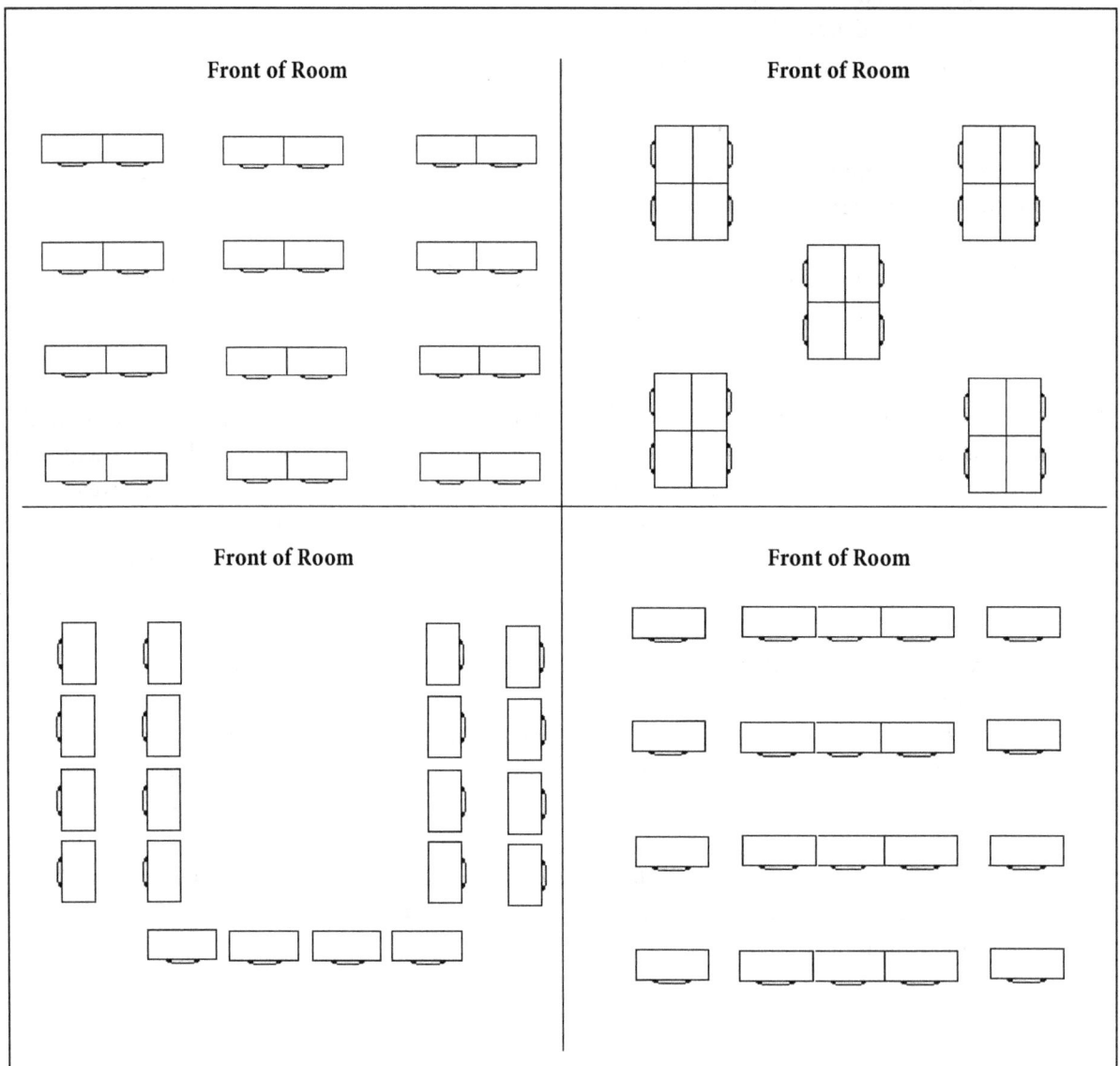

A Checklist to Plan for the First Day of School

☐ **Plan for greeting students**
Considerations: standing at the classroom door, smiling, shaking hands; posting name, welcome message, directions for sitting and/or any opening activity on the board

☐ **Plan for seating arrangement(s)**
Considerations: name plates (elementary) and folding cards can note names and be displayed on desks so that students can find their places quickly; having extra plates/cards on hand can be helpful for students who arrive and are not on the class list; alphabetical seating can help a teacher learn names

☐ **Plan for introducing self**
Considerations: a verbal welcome, review of course name, and introduction of self with a few personal details (hometown, interests, hobbies, but nothing too personal) can put students at ease

☐ **Plan for prayer on the first day**
Consideration: a specially chosen prayer can help set a positive tone for the year

☐ **Plan for getting to know students**
Considerations: taking attendance verbally to begin to learn pronunciations and nicknames; using an activity for beginning to get to know students (interest survey, sharing activity)

☐ **Plan for discussing expectations**
Considerations: introducing and discussing classroom rules (or developing them with students), reviewing school policies and emergency procedures, introducing specific classroom procedures as the need arises (i.e., introducing the procedure for passing out papers the first time a handout needs to be disseminated)

☐ **Plan for introducing course/subject**
Considerations: using an engaging activity to motivate interest in the subject, possibly passing out and introducing the textbook

☐ **Introduce the dismissal procedure**
Consideration: introducing that you dismiss the students

STUDENT SURVEY
Pick a few questions to create your own survey instrument

GENERAL QUESTIONS

1. Name
2. Birthday
3. My favorite subject
4. One thing that I am really good at is...
5. I do my best thinking when...
6. Something else that I want you to know about me is ...

RELIGION

1. What is your favorite Scripture story?
2. Who is your favorite saint? Why?
3. Name three values that are important to you.

MATHEMATICS

1. What is your lucky number? Explain how you know it is your lucky number?
2. What is your favorite game? How is math involved in it?
3. What is your most memorable mathematical experience?
4. How do you think math is related to your everyday life?

LANGUAGE ARTS

1. Where do you like to read?
2. What is the best book you read last year?
3. If you could hang out with a book character, who would it be? Why?
4. What is your favorite movie based on a book?
5. If you were to write a book, what would it be about?

SCIENCE

1. What do you think has been the most important scientific discovery? Why?
2. What is one invention that you could not live without?
3. Which science topic is most interesting to you?

SOCIAL STUDIES

1. Which historical figure would you like to interview and why?
2. What question would you ask this person?
3. If you could visit a state not previously visited, which would it be and why?
4. If you could spend time in a decade of the 1900's, which decade would you choose and why?

REVIEW OF HOMEWORK FOR _____(Period/Subject)

Dates:

#	Student Name	M	T	W	H	F	M	T	W	H	F	M	T	W	H	F	M	T	W	H	F
1																					
2																					
3																					
4																					
5																					
6																					
7																					
8																					
9																					
10																					
11																					
12																					
13																					
14																					
15																					
16																					
17																					
18																					
19																					
20																					
21																					
22																					
23																					
24																					
25																					

Key:

Reflect upon the questions offered in this section. What procedures will you establish? When will you introduce them? How will you practice them? Take time to write concrete actions for each of the following categories.

Beginning the School Day/Class Period

1. When students arrive to your classroom, will there be posted work awaiting them? If so, what will it be?
2. How will you handle tasks like documenting attendance and tardiness or taking lunch counts?
3. How will you greet students, share announcements, and facilitate prayer?

Transitions and Interruptions

1. What will your expectations be regarding how students enter the classroom? How should students move through the hallways? How will you dismiss students?

2. How will you handle requests for bathroom use, a drink of water, or pencil sharpening?

3. What are the school requirements regarding emergency drills?

During Lessons

1. How do you plan to get student attention, distribute or collect materials, collect and/or review homework, have students respond to questions (raising hands or calling out answers)?
2. How will students be expected to prepare paper headings or signal a need for help?
3. Will students be allowed to move around the room to sharpen a pencil, get a tissue or throw away a paper? If so, what parameters will you set for such movement?

Ending the School Day

1. How will students prepare for school dismissal?
2. What responsibilities for care of the classroom will they share?

Rules and Consequences 3

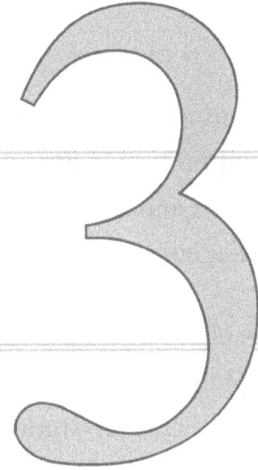

A classroom is a community. It is a space where each person should feel welcomed and accepted and where opportunity should exist for each person to contribute in positive ways. The strength of the community is actualized in certain behaviors and at the forefront is respect.

Because a classroom is communal space, rules need to exist. They identify expectations and are in place to ensure safety, productive exchanges and needed structures. Without rules and their consistent enforcement, chaos is likely to ensue. For this reason, a system of rules and consequences for infractions is a necessary function for creating a productive environment. Research shows that effective classroom management techniques show higher engagement and achievement rates for students (Marzano, 2003).

In a Catholic school setting, however, classroom management is not simply a means to attaining higher engagement and achievement rates. Catholic schools have a responsibility to develop moral and ethical students attentive to Gospel values and mindful of their responsibility as members of the Christian community.

As a teacher considers classroom management decisions, attention to Church teachings, the needs of individual students, and opportunities for moral and character development can help guide choices made.

WHAT RESEARCH SAYS

- Communal organization is a key characteristic of effective Catholic high schools. Integral to this organization are shared values about school purpose, student capabilities and norms of behavior, shared activities, and social relations that emphasize collegiality and extended teacher roles (Bryk, Lee, & Holland, 1993).

- Teachers who have solid relationships with their students have fewer management problems (Brown, 2003; R. Marzano, 2003; R. Marzano & J. Marzano, 2003). Effective teacher-student relationships are characterized by a combination of appropriate levels of dominance (defined as ability to provide clear purpose and strong guidance related to academics and student behavior) and cooperation (defined as concern for the needs of others and desire to function as a part of a team; R. Marzano, 2003; R. Marzano & J. Marzano, 2003; Wubbels, Levy, & Brekelmans, 1997).

- Effective classroom management techniques in urban settings include showing care and developing trust in relationships with students, being assertive and explicitly stating expectations for behavior and academic growth, and listening to students and attending to their verbal and non-verbal means of communication (Brown, 2003).

- Disruptions occur in all classrooms but are fewer in those in which teachers utilize effective disciplinary interventions (R. Marzano, 2003). The most effective interventions include a combination of rewards for acceptable behavior and consequences for unacceptable behavior.

CONSIDERATIONS FOR RULES AND CONSEQUENCES

A number of factors contribute to managing the classroom environment successfully: well-planned lessons that are highly engaging and actively involve students, positive teacher-student relationships, and a clearly stated set of rules and consequences that are implemented with consistency. Well-planned lessons will be the topic of chapter 4. This section briefly revisits the teacher-student relationship introduced within chapter 1 and then considers more closely the development and implementation of classroom rules and consequences.

The Teacher-Student Relationship

Showing respect to all students. Treating students with respect helps to solidify the teacher-student relationship which in turn is likely to have a positive impact on classroom management. Students want to know that their teachers care about them and will often work harder for teachers from whom they experience respect. Respectful actions and responses not only strengthen the teacher-student relationship, they provide important modeling for students. Students are more likely to respond in kind when they experience respect from their teachers.

Respectful attitudes include recognition and development of potential, and acknowledgement and consideration for feelings and preferences. Each student deserves personalized attention, but a teacher must also be careful to not show favoritism. Students will not respond positively if they perceive that one or a few students are privileged and treated differently.

> *"Even students who are very young can sense whether the atmosphere in the school is pleasant or not. They are more willing to cooperate when they feel respected, trusted and loved. And their willingness to cooperate will be reinforced by a school climate which is warm and friendly, when teachers are ready to help, and when they find it easy to get along with the other students"* (Congregation for Catholic Education [CCE], 1988, §106).

Examples in Action

- Greeting students by name as they arrive to the classroom.

- Using body language to communicate interest (a smile and a handshake can communicate warmth, eye contact and nodding can communicate understanding).

- Getting to know individual student's interests outside of school by asking about them and/or attending events meaningful to the students (sporting events, musical performances, etc.).

- Taking time to listen to student concerns.

- Following through on commitments made to students.

- Treating students equally.

- Including ways for students to share about their culture and opportunities to celebrate diversity (a special prayer service, topical discussion to highlight culturally significant feast days and holidays).

Creating classroom community. Creating a sense of community in the classroom flows from respect and encourages a respectful environment. A caring classroom community builds relationships among students, gives students voice, fosters responsibility, and acknowledges the importance of each classroom member.

Attention to moral character development is an important consideration for building the classroom community and for managing the classroom. According to Lickona and Davidson (2005), moral character is a relational orientation that "enables us to treat others—and ourselves—with respect and care and to act with integrity" (p. 18). When students come to value their membership in the community and see how their actions and choices impact it, they are better able to make positive choices regarding behavior in the classroom.

Examples in Action

- Assigning responsibilities to students to share in the care of the classroom (care of classroom pet or plant, distributing or collecting materials, etc.).

- Complimenting individuals for their unique contributions within the classroom community; emphasizing Gospel values; affirming positive traits and actions as they are demonstrated.

- Showing care for each individual member of the class community (a prayer intercession for a student who is ill, a note or e-mail to a student out for an extended period of time, a special greeting to a student returning from an absence, an inquiry about a family member of a student who is ill or in the hospital, etc.).

- Celebrating within the classroom community (acknowledging a birthday, a seasonal event, a student success in a sport, etc.).

- Holding morning meetings in elementary classrooms and advisory sessions in middle/high school classrooms to make communal decisions and/or come to resolutions about class problems.

- Discussing with students concrete ways in which integrity and respect can be compromised (the impact of cheating, stealing from classmates, etc.).

- Involving elementary students in the development of classroom rules and/or involving elementary students in presenting scenarios that demonstrate the benefit of classroom rules.

Being assertive. Contributing to positive relationships is the perception by students of teacher assertiveness. Research shows that students prefer assertive teachers who speak clearly about expectations, consistently enforce them, and provide strong guidance (Wubbels et al., 1997). Assertive teachers display legitimate command and an appropriate level of seriousness, and they demonstrate responsible action in a consistent and firm manner.

The notion of firmness is often misunderstood by first-year teachers who want to be liked and do not want to be perceived negatively by students. Firmness does not equate with harshness or unkindness; rather it is associated with consistency with expectations and a readiness to address matters of concern promptly and fairly.

Examples in Action

- Attending to inappropriate behavior and not ignoring it.

- Speaking calmly yet firmly as needed.

- Matching facial expression with content of the message being spoken.

- Using appropriate tone of voice to convey message.

- Maintaining professional boundaries and not showing favoritism to any students.

Classroom Management

This section considers the development and implementation of rules and consequences.

Developing rules. When developing rules, it is important to limit the number of rules and focus them on the most essential expectations regarding behavior and conduct. If a long list of rules is developed, students might struggle to recall them. If the language is confusing or is not developmentally appropriate, students might struggle to understand them. If a list of "do nots" is created (i.e., do not write on desks, do not speak while a classmate is speaking), students might struggle to appreciate the values emphasized through the rules (respect for property and others). Five simple and positively-stated rules that can be easily recalled works well.

In elementary classrooms, involving children in coming up with rules promotes children's moral development (DeVries & Zan, 2003) and reinforces the notion of the classroom as a community. Furthermore, it is generally reasoned that involving children in coming up with classroom rules increases their likelihood of following rules because they have invested in creating them. Involving children in developing rules is a valid approach but a teacher should not undertake this naively. Children will only honor a created list of rules if their teacher enforces them in a firm and consistent manner.

Such an approach to the development of rules can occur in middle school and/or high school classrooms as well. However, it may be less practical to involve students in setting classroom rules because different groups of students are moving in and out of the classroom throughout the school day.

In whatever way rules are set, it remains important that they are compatible with Church teachings, Gospel values, the school's mission, and schoolwide policies.

Sample Classroom Rules

HIGH SCHOOL

- Respect self and others.
- Come to class prepared and on time.
- Raise your hand when wanting to speak.
- Show respect for class materials and all school property.
- Follow school rules.

Science Teacher

- Follow all school rules.
- Respect your teacher, classmates, all property, and most importantly yourself.
- Raise your hand to speak in class.
- Have all materials present and prepared before class begins.

Math Teacher

- Respect yourself, your peers, and other people's property.
- Speak and act appropriately at all times.
- Follow all school rules.
- Come to class punctually and prepared.

Foreign Language Teacher

MIDDLE SCHOOL

- Always arrive to class on time and prepared to learn.
- Listen to others when they are speaking.
- Keep your desk and lab area clean and organized.
- Respect the classroom community.

Science Teacher

- Be respectful.
- Raise your hand to speak; listen when others are speaking.
- Arrive on time, prepared to learn.
- Follow the teacher's instructions at all times.
- School-wide rules are in effect in and out of the classroom.

Language Arts Teacher

- Follow the teacher's instructions at all times.
- Respect yourself, others, and property.
- Be punctual and prepared.
- Stay on task.
- Follow all school rules.

Social Studies Teacher

ELEMENTARY SCHOOL

- Be respectful towards others and their property.
- Follow teacher directions.
- Be kind.
- Be honest in all you do and say.
- Be safe.

Grade 4 Teacher

- Follow all school rules.
- Follow classroom procedures.
- Treat others as you want to be treated.
- Listen when others are talking.
- Keep your hands, feet, and objects to yourself.

Grade 3 Teacher

- Be respectful of others.
- Listen carefully and follow directions.
- Keep hands, feet, and materials to yourself.
- Always try your best.

Grade 2 Teacher

Sharing rules. Rules should be shared on day one of the school year. They should be explained thoroughly so that students are clear about expectations. Once introduced, the rules should be implemented immediately.

When rules are introduced, it is important to check for understanding. A teacher should not assume that all students will explain a stated rule in the same way. Taking time to discuss the rules, clarify their meaning, and allow for questions are important practices to undertake so that all students are clear about the rules and their intended meaning.

Examples in Action

- Teaching and reinforcing rules through discussions about their usefulness and meaning; utilizing role plays to help students fully comprehend their meaning.

- Posting classroom rules where they can be easily viewed.

- Sharing rules with parents in writing (newsletter or parent letter).

Implementing consequences when needed. According to Hudson (2006) discipline in the Catholic school setting can be understood in light of discipleship. He writes that both words come from the Latin word *disculpus*, meaning to teach, and suggests an opportunity to teach is provided when disciplining students. Such a mindset helps the teacher to "look at discipline as relational and within a religious framework" (p. 37).

Every classroom teacher is likely to face disruptive behavior but how a teacher handles such a disruption can determine long-term management effectiveness or ineffectiveness. Respectful actions that contribute towards effectiveness are attentiveness, consistency, and assertiveness.

Attentiveness to student needs helps to keep students feeling secure. Typical student needs for dignity, belonging, and power can be met through simple actions of respect revealed in informal interactions, opportunities for shared responsibilities, and involvement in decision making when appropriate. Attentiveness also relates to careful monitoring of all that is occurring in the classroom and at all times.

Consistency refers to attending to matters of concern and doing so similarly with all students. Respect is implicit in such actions and students recognize fairness when rules are implemented with consistency.

Assertiveness, as previously noted, describes firmness in monitoring expectations and prompt attention to unacceptable behavior. A teacher might experience feelings of frustration in having to address a behavioral matter, but it remains important that such feelings are not shown when relating to the student. Addressing the matter calmly yet assertively will allow the student to maintain dignity and the relationship to remain intact. At such times, always describe the behavior as unacceptable, not the student.

> *"Most of all, students should be able to recognize authentic human qualities in their teachers. They are teachers of the faith; however, like Christ, they must also be teachers of what it means to be human. This includes culture, but it also includes such things as affection, tact, understanding, serenity of spirit, a balanced judgment, patience in listening to others and prudence in the way they respond, and, finally, availability for personal meetings and conversations with the students. A teacher who has a clear vision of the Christian milieu and lives in accord with it will be able to help young people develop a similar vision, and will give them the inspiration they need to put it into practice"* (CCE, 1988, §96).

Examples in Action

To monitor classroom behavior

- Using proximity/moving around classroom while teaching.
- Making eye contact with students and holding gaze upon an offending student.
- Allowing silence to speak.
- Using cues that have an understood predetermined meaning such as raising a hand in the air to signal for attention and silence.
- Avoiding turning one's back to students. If needing to write at the board, practice doing so with body half turned with an eye towards the board and the other towards the class.
- Emphasizing choice with students (if you choose to do unacceptable behavior, you choose a predetermined consequence).
- Being aware that some students will test boundaries and it is important to act promptly.

To address misbehavior

- Indicating to student to stop specific behavior: verbal reminder, direct and succinct
- Speaking to the offending student in private.
- Avoiding arguing with the student especially in front of other students.
- Developing a series of progressive consequences as noted in the following examples taken from management plans.

Sample Management Plan Statements
Negative Consequences Examples

HIGH SCHOOL

1. Verbal warning: "Consider yourself warned."
2. Detention during lunch or after school.
3. Phone call to parents.
4. Conference with parents.
5. Report sent to principal's office for other disciplinary action.

MIDDLE SCHOOL

Level One
- Look at student while continuing to teach.
- Walk near student while continuing to teach (without putting back to whole class).
- Pause in teaching for one moment and stare at student.
- Pause in teaching for one moment, stare, and use student's name quickly. Then return to teaching.
- Quietly walk over to student and ask them if there is a problem.

Level Two
- Publicly address the situation with student's name, asking if there is a problem, asking if they know why I am addressing him or her.
- Now, the student receives one formal verbal warning.

Level Three
- If problems continue, and behavior is disruptive to the entire class, students may be sent to the following places depending on nature of disruption: another teacher's classroom, the office. This is considered the second formal warning. Being sent out of the classroom also warrants a conversation between the teacher and the student at the end of the day. This may also warrant a call home to parents depending on the nature of the disruption.

Level Four
- If the student returns and continues to be disruptive, the student may receive a detention. Detentions are administered Tuesday, Wednesday, and Thursday after school for 45 minutes. Students will be given a note explaining the detention, and a call will also be made to the parents notifying them of the detention.

Beyond
- If student behavior does not change after talk or detention, call home again.
- If student behavior does not change after a call home and all previous steps, the principal will become more directly involved, including spending time at the office if there are continued disruptions or in-school suspensions.
- If none of these methods work, or if a student exhibits explicit, relentless defiance or creates a classroom environment where absolutely no teaching or learning can take place, make the situation known to the principal.

Negative Consequences Examples (continued)

ELEMENTARY SCHOOL

Grade 2 Example

I will assign each student a number and place numbered envelopes with stoplight symbol cards (red, yellow, green) for each one. The following procedure will then be applied if a rule is broken:

- Verbal warning
- Move to yellow: lose 5 minutes of recess
- Move to red: no recess, note home
- Already on red and break another rule: spend some time in 3rd grade or with principal (depending on offense)

Behavior color will be reported to parents each day as the student checks off his or her behavior on a homework sheet for the week.

Grade 5 Example

- I will use the method of giving a verbal warning to the student. Each student will get one warning a day.
- On the next offense, the student will be sent to the refocus desk in the back of the room to fill out a refocus sheet. The refocus sheet asks the student to reflect on how behavior is affecting his or her ability to achieve goals.
- For the third offense, the student will be sent to the refocus desk in the other fifth grade room. I also will send the student home with a behavior report that the student and I will fill out, describing what happened, why it is wrong, what could have been done differently, and a plan to change the behavior. The student will need to return the form signed by a parent.
- For the fourth offense the student will be sent to the office, and I will call the student's home.

When a matter is deemed serious and a consequence warranted, a process involving communication-correction-consequence is important. *Communication* allows for a discussion of the student's actions with opportunity for the student to explain choices and consider alternatives. The communication incorporates *correction* which is a review of expectations and ends with a meaningful *consequence* given.

Just as it is important to act promptly to address matters of concern, it is equally important to provide feedback and reinforcement to the students about behavior. There is much debate about the limited value of extrinsic rewards but they are generally proven to provide incentive to students (R. Marzano, 2003). A general rule of thumb when using rewards is to limit them and to emphasize intrinsic motivators such as the satisfaction one feels for giving one's best effort and for work well done. As students mature, they generally become more intrinsically motivated so fewer tangible rewards are likely to be needed during the high school years.

There are four other details that are important to remember when choosing rewards. First, if rewards are too easy or too difficult to achieve they are not likely to be effective. Second, not all rewards will be perceived favorably by every student. Some students like verbal praise; for others it is a source of tension as they don't like being signaled out and might get teased by peers. Third, it often works well to involve students in coming up with potential rewards. This helps to generate a list of rewards that are very meaningful to the specific group of students. Fourth, students often respond to novelty. Changes to positive rewards and unique and clever ideas tend to excite students and encourage positive behavior.

Examples in Action

All Levels
- Using non-tangible rewards: smiles, thumbs up, positive comments on papers, handshakes, high fives, verbal recognition, group applause.

Middle Grades
- Using tangible rewards: in some settings, stickers and certificates are appreciated.
- Using group rewards: a pizza party or a physical activity like shooting baskets with the teacher might be well received.

Elementary Grades
- Using tangible rewards: stickers, certificates, prayer cards/medals, school-related items like themed pencils and erasers, tickets towards a prize (prizes might include lunch with teacher, earning minutes on the classroom computers, earning minutes for use of centers).
- Using group rewards: the approach might be to utilize a jar to which marbles are added and when full the class earns a prize. Board tallies can be utilized in a similar manner. Actual rewards might include the reading of a book chosen by the students, minutes for use of centers, or a game of kickball with the teacher.

Sample Management Plan Statements
Positive Consequences Examples

HIGH SCHOOL

- Verbal praise from teacher.
- Written praise and words of encouragement from teacher.
- Conversation with principal on positive attributes of student.
- Call home to praise positive attributes of student.

MIDDLE SCHOOL

- Give verbal praise and smiles.
- Write notes of encouragement or recognition on homework, quizzes, and tests.
- If near a student's parent after school in the parking lot or at a sporting event, praise the student so that the parent can hear. Also, giving direct praise to the parent about the student is another option.
- Notes or calls home to the parents with words of praise about the student.
- If a student is punished and appears to grow from experience, compliment student.

ELEMENTARY SCHOOL

Grade 2 Example
- I will have a board directly below the chalkboard, with a road stretching from a school on one side to a destination such as a pizza party or popcorn party. I will have a school bus cut-out which signifies our journey together as a class. At the end of each school day as we pack up, I will move the bus forward a space if the class behaved and worked well that day, reviewing specific examples of good behavior as well as pointing out any shortcomings we can work on together. Once the bus reaches its destination (hopefully about every 2 weeks) the students will receive a reward, such as a pencil, eraser, extra reading time, a special game, or some time outside, and then we will begin the journey together again to a new destination.

Grade 5 Example
- When the class is behaving well as a group I will place some marbles into a jar. When the jar gets full, I will give the class some kind of reward such as a fun game inside or a game of kickball outside that I will participate in. The marbles will carry over each week; I will never take marbles out of the jar because the students have earned them.
- I will reward individuals for their good behavior with frequent praise and words of encouragement. Also, for good behavior the students will get raffle tickets. At the end of each day I will draw a raffle ticket. The winner will be able to select a prize from the prize basket.
- I will also mark down each day which "group" (aisle) in the room behaved the best. The winning group from the previous day will be allowed to sit on the carpet during silent reading. Each student in the group who won the most days at the end of the week will get a raffle ticket.

High School Teaching

Second only to one's identity as a Catholic teacher is how one acts in the classroom and manages a classroom. In this, one must attempt to balance the infinitely difficult standard of God the Father in being infinitely just and infinitely merciful. Too much of either is unbalanced and unhealthy for the development of our students. Essential to making this lofty goal more accessible is a firm set of procedures, rules, and standards in the classroom. These should allow you to be consistent in enforcing discipline, but also flexible enough to be both merciful and understanding of your students. A general suggestion would be to always put great value in the individual and group teacher-student relationships. Just as our Trinitarian God is a God of relationship, relationships are of primary importance in a truly Catholic education. This does not mean always being "nice" to your students, if being nice means failing to enforce policies and sacrificing consistency and discipline in your classroom. It is possible, however, to be a benevolent disciplinarian. Think of the love of a parent. The parent scolds, but the child should always know without the least bit of doubt that the parent has infinite love for the child.

— *Anthony D'Agostino*

Make sure the consequences fit the "crime". Nothing will destroy your credibility with a student or damage the way he or she responds to you more than responding in an unjust way. Remember that you are helping form the student who broke the rule, and as such, consequences are teaching moments. Explain the situation to the student and talk about it in a calm, clear, understanding manner. Help the student understand what he or she did, why it was wrong, what the consequence is, and why that is the consequence you have chosen. This will help form studenbts in their own responsibility, but also they will understand the process, and hopefully be able to better judge their actions, avoiding future consequences down the road.

— *Matt Reichert*

Quickly and quietly is the best way to handle classroom disruptions. Students are not looking to see so much what you say, but more what you do. Always follow up on any consequences you say you will give. If you know you won't have enough follow-through to give the consequence, don't even threaten. Pray for your students that misbehave, and imagine that they are your younger brothers and sisters, especially when you are tempted to lose patience with them.

— *Noah Beacom*

Middle School Teaching

My first year of teaching, I had six rules; however, none of my students could remember more than three. This past year, I have made only three rules and these are my mantra in my classroom: respect, responsibility, and integrity. If a student has a behavior problem, which means that he/she has had a warning and a second warning, the third results in a consequence for a lunch detention. The student needs to complete a sheet that asks he/she did not follow the classroom agreements and how he/she will correct behavior. I then have a discussion after class with the student about a consequence, whether it is a call to a parent or a lunch detention.

— *Rory Dippold*

In my first year of teaching, I was much too nice. Students took advantage of this, and it became very difficult to correct after the first month or two as a teacher. In my second year, every action had a consequence, and students learned this from day one. As a result, I had control of the classroom and had significantly less discipline problems and disruptions than the previous year. Another good idea is to get students to help create the classroom rules. Of course, you are going to get some ridiculous stuff—"All students can have their shirts untucked" or "Students can chew gum whenever they want"—but you will also get some serious responses. Guide students through this to create some great rules as a group. This allows students to buy in, as they helped create the rules that govern their classroom.

— Brett Guy

Consequences must match the offense—always. If they misbehave in the hallway, then they lose hallway privileges at all times except between classes. *— Matt Houlihan*

The students love this reward system! I have "Gotcha Gold" cards that I use to help students, who have demonstrated an exemplary job on a project, did a deed that was extraordinary, or followed directions the first time asked. I provide a reward for these students at the end of each month with a raffle for prizes. At the beginning of the year, I hand a letter on school letterhead soliciting help from local businesses to donate certificates for the raffle. Your best success will be businesses that already have a partnership with the school. The gift certificates from a variety of places make the students look forward to the last day in the month! *— Rory Dippold*

One idea I came up with when I first started teaching was the "Behavior First and Ten." Other teachers and educators at my new school have adopted it and like it too, so it works for a lot of people. Basically it is a football field (100 yards) that has football helmets attached by magnets or Velcro. When students do something well as a class like lining up or doing bell work right away, the helmet moves up ten yards. When they don't follow the rules and procedures, the helmet moves back ten yards. It is a great visual for the students and helps community building as the students try to get a touchdown for a class treat or positive outcome. Above all, consistency is the most important thing. If you consistently uphold them to the same rules and consequences and high standards each day, students will respond. It takes time to develop that realization sometimes for the students, and a day or two of consequences won't fix problems in the classroom. Students want to be held to high standards and will respond if you keep the bar high. You just have to be patient for them to respond to it. *— Katie Key*

Elementary School Teaching

In addition to my "card-pulling" system, I also had an "I'm Sorry Board." If a student did something wrong to another student that did not warrant a pulled card, they would have to pull a suggestion from the "I'm Sorry Board." They would then have to follow through with what was on the card they picked (in addition to apologizing to the student). These included a handshake, a pat on the back, a hug, a high-five, etc. *— Katie Cawley*

I use the card system (green, yellow, red) in my second grade classroom. This system works very well for the majority of students. However, almost every year there has been one or two students who needed to have this system modified. An easy way to do this is to add another color to their chart or to break up the day into segments, (i.e., morning to recess, recess to lunch, and after lunch). This modified behavior chart lets all children have success and achieve a "green" day! *— Clare Murphy*

I liked using green, yellow, and red zones for positive and negative consequences. In one class I had to show it on the board (I used clothespins to move a student from one zone to another). In another class I would just tell them if they switched zones. Each day they were in green they were entered into the end of the week raffle. At the end of the week I would draw three names. The incentive for the students was the more green zone days you had, the greater chance you had to win a prize. I used recess time as a negative consequence. The most important thing was being on top of everything from the beginning and making sure the class was run in a way that everyone could learn and everyone felt comfortable.

— *Brynn Johnson*

I have a stop light in my room, which is created out of colored plates. Students begin the day on green. Yellow is a warning. Students who move to red or black complete a form, which will be returned the next day. Below is a copy of the Traffic Form. The actual form has a picture of a stop light.

Write in COMPLETE SENTENCES!!!   DATE: _____

(1) Today I chose to move my pin from GREEN to: RED BLACK because I _____

---

(2) I BROKE THE FOLLOWING RULE: 1. Respect yourself, others, and the property of others. 2. Raise your hand and wait patiently for the teacher to call on you. 3. Be responsible! Work must be neat, complete and on-time. 4. Follow directions and listen attentively. 5. Use self-control! Stay in your seat until the teacher gives you permission to move.

(3) Next time I will_____

Signatures:

My Signature _____

Teacher's _____

Parent's _____

Due tomorrow!

More information: 1. YELLOW = Warning; 5 minutes of walking at recess. 2. RED = completed Traffic Form signed by teacher and parent. 3. BLACK = second completed Traffic form signed by teacher and parent; 5 additional minutes of walking at recess. Student's desk may be moved to a "safe spot."

— *Courtney Jianas Vogtner*

REFERENCES

Brown, D. (2003). Urban teachers' use of culturally responsive management strategies. *Theory into Practice, 42*(4), 277-282.

Bryk, A. S., Lee, V. E., & Holland, P. B. (1993). *Catholic schools and the common good.* Cambridge, MA: Harvard University Press.

Congregation for Catholic Education. (1988). *The religious dimension of education in a Catholic school.* Washington, DC: United States Catholic Conference.

Davidson, M., Lickona, T., & Lickona, T. (2007). Smart & good. *Independent School, 66*(2), 24-30.

DeVries, R., & Zan, B. (2003). When children make rules. *Educational Leadership, 61*(1), 64-67.

Hudson, W. (2006). Relationships as the basis of discipline. *Today's Catholic Teacher, 40*(2), 37-40.

Lickona, T., & Davidson, M. (2005). *Smart & good high schools: Integrating excellence and ethics for success in school work and beyond.* Cortland, NY: Center for the 4th and 5th Rs (Respect & Responsibility)/Washington, DC: Character Education Partnership.

Marzano, R. (2003). *Classroom management that works: Research-based strategies for every teacher.* Alexandria, VA: Association for Supervision and Curriculum Development.

Marzano, R., & Marzano, J. (2003). The key to classroom management. *Educational Leadership, 61*(1), 6-13.

Wubbels, T., Levy, J., & Brekelmans, M. (1997). Paying attention to relationships. *Educational Leadership, 54*(7), 82-86.

DAILY COMMUNICATION SHEET

Student _____

Week of _____

Day	Teacher's Comment	Parent Signature
Monday		
Tuesday		
Wednesday		
Thursday		
Friday		

BEHAVIOR REFLECTION SHEET

Date: _____

This is what happened:

This is what I could have done differently:

My plan to change is:

Student signature: _____Teacher signature: _____

Parent signature and date: _____
(Comments)

BEHAVIOR UPDATE

Week of _____

Student _____

	Teacher:	Teacher:	Teacher:	Teacher:
M				
T				
W				
H				
F				

Total points for the week _____

Teacher signature _____

Parent signature _____

Comments:

Key:
3 = satisfactory
2 = needs improvement
1 = unsatisfactory

BEHAVIOR LOG

Student _____

Date/Time	Behavior Observed	Action Taken

PARENT/GUARDIAN CONTACT LOG

Date/ Time	Student	Form of Contact *e-mail, telephone call, informal meeting, formal meeting*	Details *who initiated contact, reason, agreed upon resolution, pertinent details*

CREATING YOUR MANAGEMENT PLAN
Rules and Consequences

Reflect upon the rules and consequences you would like to implement for the successful management of your classroom. Take time to write ideas for each of these questions.

1. How do you plan to develop strong relationships with your students? List at least 3-5 concrete actions you will take.
2. What are the 3-5 rules you plan to establish within your classroom?
    a. How will rules be developed? Introduced?
    b. What are positive consequences you hope to implement?
    c.. What are negative consequences you plan to implement?

Classroom Time

4

Utilizing time effectively in the classroom directly relates to instructional planning. The teacher who is well-planned and works to develop meaningful lessons is more likely to engage students fully during lesson implementation and thus manage the environment successfully.

There are numerous resources available to help in the area of planning—school curriculum, textbooks, supplementary materials, colleagues, on-line resources—but a teacher must use these resources discriminately in order to attend to the specific needs and interests of his/her students. This latter point is especially significant. Instructional planning is a context-dependent activity and must take into consideration pupil characteristics and needs while attending to state and/or diocesan standards.

In a Catholic school, one further consideration is most relevant. According to Miller (2006) who summarizes the Holy See's teaching on Catholic schools, one essential mark of a Catholic school is that it is imbued with a Catholic worldview throughout its curriculum. In a Catholic school,

> there is no separation between time for learning and time for formation, between acquiring notions and growing in wisdom. The various school subjects do not present only knowledge to be attained, but also values to be acquired and truths to be discovered. (Congregation for Catholic Education [CCE], 1997, §14)

It is important when instructional planning to keep in mind that "religious values and motivation are [to be] cultivated in all subject areas and, indeed, in all of the various activities going on in the school" (CCE, 1988, §107).

Planning is key to effective instruction. A careful process of planning contributes to teacher comfort with content, organization of material, and most importantly the purpose and direction of the instruction. Thorough planning and effective lesson implementation strengthened by appropriate pacing and smooth transitions will allow the time in the classroom to remain purposeful and productive.

WHAT RESEARCH SAYS

Research related to instructional planning shows that:

- Effective teachers identify clear objectives and match assessments and instructional strategies appropriately (Stronge, 2007).

- When structuring lessons, a number of strategies contribute to coherent instruction: determining one main learning goal; communicating the lesson's purpose; choosing content and activities matched to the learning goal and sequencing them appropriately; linking content ideas and activities and clearly noting to students the important links; and summarizing and synthesizing important ideas (Roth & Garnier, 2006).

Brain-based research relevant to classroom instruction reveals that:

- Several factors influence attention that students give to newly arriving information and these include novelty (the brain is naturally attentive to something that is unusual), intensity (the brain generally responds to more intense stimuli), and movement (the brain responds to stimuli that move; Wolfe, 2001).

- Two factors contribute to sustained attention: meaning (students are more likely to attend to new information if their brains can connect it to information previously received and if the material holds relevance for them) and emotion (brains are programmed to attend more to emotionally charged information; Wolfe, 2001; McGeehan, 2001).

- The brain is designed for fluctuation rather than long, sustained attention and focus. The length of concentration that can be sustained is normally between 10-12 minutes (slightly less for younger students and slightly more for older students; Jensen, 2005).

Regarding time and learning, research shows:

- There is little or no relationship between allocated time (time spent in school) and student achievement, some relationship between engaged time (time on task) and student achievement, and a greater relationship between academic learning time (the period during which an instructional activity matches a student's readiness to learn and results in actual learning) and student achievement (Aronson, Zimmerman, & Carlos, 1998, 2001; Zimmerman, 2001).

- In a study of how instructional minutes were used in 15 high school classrooms, students were engaged in waiting about 17% of the time (Fisher, 2009). Other research shows that as much as 30% of class time is used for non-instructional purposes (Stronge, 2007).

CONSIDERATIONS FOR SPENDING CLASSROOM TIME WELL

Instructional Planning

Well-planned lessons are essential for making the most of instructional minutes. When planning for classroom instruction there are many important considerations. Three essential areas are attention to state and diocesan standards, consideration of pupil characteristics and needs, and organization of quality lessons.

Attention to state and diocesan standards. Standards—whether national, state, or diocesan—define expectations of what students will know and be able to do within the various content areas. They are an important resource that gives direction for curriculum development and classroom teaching. Standards provide structure but also allow individual creativity for teachers in choices regarding instructional strategies and assessments.

When planning, an alignment between mandated standards and curriculum, instruction and assessment must be evident. Alignment is more than a teacher reading a standard and noting that "yes, I teach that." Alignment must look at content, skills, understandings, and processes expressed through standards to determine if teaching strategies and assessments are addressing the standard in the most appropriate ways. According to Drake and Burns (2004) both external alignment (the local curriculum aligns with mandated or suggested standards) and internal alignment (the content and intent of the standards appropriately matches instructional strategies and assessments) need to occur.

Examples in Action

- Reviewing state and/or diocesan standards before the school year begins and referencing them within all lesson development.

- Making connections among the big ideas of the subject area to facilitate more coherent instruction.

Consideration of pupil characteristics and needs. Catholic schools celebrate and appreciate the diversity of their students—ethnic, racial, religious, language, gender, and physical. Each of these areas adds to the uniqueness of the individual and contributes to the overall dynamics of the classroom environment.

Differences also abound in ability and how students learn. In terms of instruction, students possess diverse learning styles, that is, preferences for taking in new information, learning new skills, and processing learning.

Because of the diversity in learning preferences, it is important to plan multiple activities to engage students in a variety of ways. Research shows that a combination of graphical representations that illustrate key concepts and processes and verbal description of those concepts and processes facilitates student learning (Pashler et al., 2007).

> "Any genuine educational philosophy has to be based on the nature of the human person, and therefore must take into account all of the physical and spiritual powers of each individual, along with the call of each one to be an active and creative agent in service to society. And this philosophy must be open to a religious dimension. Human beings are fundamentally free; they are not the property of the state or of any human organization. The entire process of education, therefore, is a service to the individual students, helping each one to achieve the most complete formation possible" (CCE, 1988, §63).

Examples in Action

- Taking time at the start of the year to find out student characteristics and learning preferences through surveys, pre-tests, oral questioning, or writing activities.

- Varying instructional methods to meet the needs of all learners; in addition to oral presentation, including visual aids and movement activities to maximize learning.

- Actively involving students in the lesson; asking questions, using peer exchanges, utilizing small group activities, using writing or drawing activities.

- Varying levels of difficulty in learning; asking both lower level and high level questions throughout a lesson.

- Providing opportunities for remediation and enrichment.

Organization of quality lessons. When planning lessons, it is essential to have an objective in mind. Objectives are statements that describe the intended learning as a result of instruction. Objectives guide the lesson. Once stated, decisions about assessment and instruction can be made.

Bloom's Taxonomy of Cognitive Processes (Bloom, 1956) provides a useful frame of reference for writing objectives. Each of the six categories of knowledge, comprehension, application, analysis, synthesis, and evaluation has certain descriptive verbs associated with it that emphasize particular intellectual abilities and skills. The more complex the learning process, the more likely the learning outcome will hold student interest, increase retention, and have greater transfer value (Grolund, 2004).

Objectives should be stated in clear and specific terms and should point to observable student outcomes. When preparing to write an objective, consider the process (verb) that best represents the intellectual activity the students are to perform and write the objective in the form, students will be able to . . . (abbreviated to SWBAT). Examples of objectives include the following:

SWBAT identify family-related vocabulary.
> Middle School Spanish lesson; KNOWLEDGE level objective

SWBAT explain how the climate, culture, and economy of an area affects where people choose to live.
> Elementary Social Studies lesson; COMPREHENSION level objective

SWBAT multiply a two digit number by a one digit multiplier.
> Elementary Math lesson; APPLICATION level objective

SWBAT analyze electrostatic forces and the flow of current through a simple circuit.
> High School Science lesson; ANALYSIS level objective

SWBAT compose a poem using various types of figurative language.
> Middle School Language Arts lesson; SYNTHESIS level objective

SWBAT evaluate the theme of forgiveness in the Prodigal Son parable against Jesus' own actions and relate to their own lives.
> High School Theology lesson; EVALUATION level objective

Once an objective has been chosen, structuring the lesson can occur, taking into consideration assessments first and then instructional strategies in a backwards design process (Wiggins & McTighe, 1998). A simple but essential planning guide poses three questions: (1) What will students know and be able to do by the end of the lesson? (2) How will it be determined that students have achieved the objective? (3) What teaching strategies and instructional tasks can help students achieve the objective? See Figure 2.

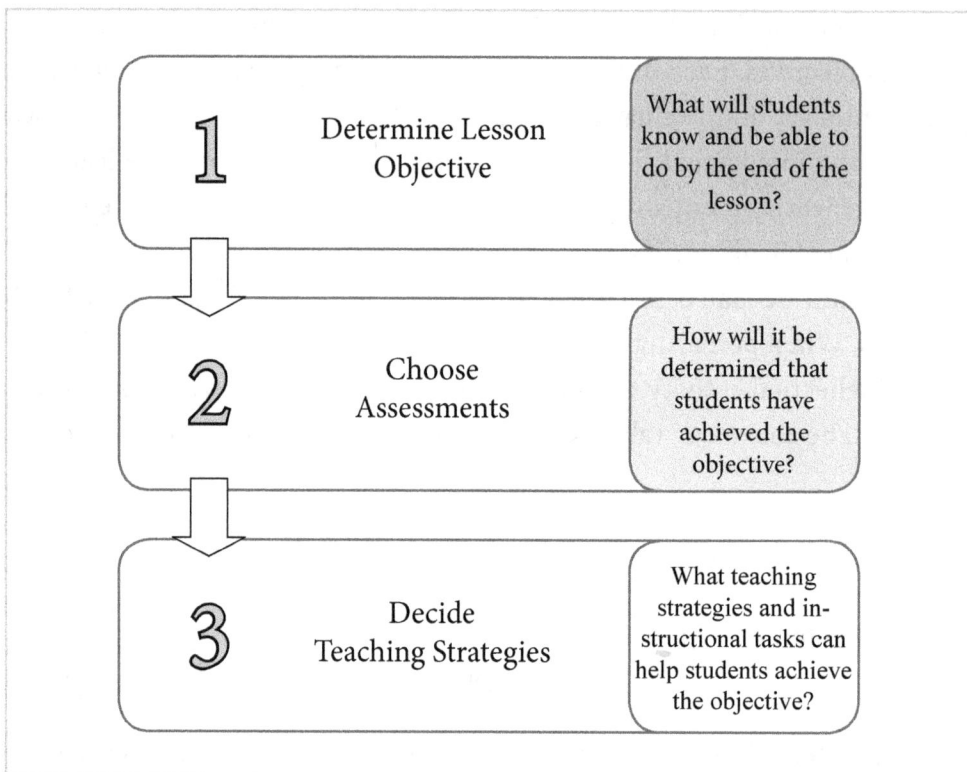

Figure 2. Instructional Process

An important consideration is the number of days needed for the lesson to be most effective. In order to help students make connections among ideas, lesson plans are typically 2-4 day experiences.

There are various ways to structure a lesson but most generally include a dynamic opening aimed at capturing student attention, various instructional activities, ongoing assessment, and closure. These essential considerations in planning lessons are explained in Table 2.

To open lessons, effective teachers enhance the learning readiness of their students in such ways as making the lesson objective known, connecting the current lesson to previous learning, arousing student interest and curiosity, and using advance organizers and questions to prepare students for learning (Cotton, 2000). To facilitate instruction and to meet the needs of all learners, a variety of well chosen activities that might include auditory practices (such as questioning or a brief lecture), use of visuals (graphic representations, pictures), and hands-on approaches (demonstrations, labs, use of manipulatives) is important. The goal of instruction is to help students move toward eventual independent practice. Assessment is noted as following the instructional phase but is actually interwoven throughout a lesson as a teacher uses questions, observation, and written work to inform instructional decisions. More formal lesson assessment is likely to occur at the end of the lesson and determines if the lesson's objective has been met. A period of closure should be included on every day of the lesson and will typically involve some type of assessment to determine what students have learned on that day.

Table 2. *Essential Considerations in Planning Lessons*

Essential Considerations	Questions to Consider	Samples of Effective Strategies
MOTIVATIONAL SET *generate interest in the lesson*	What will help to capture student interest in the lesson? How can you connect their prior knowledge with new information to be presented in the lesson?	• KWL (What do I know, want to know, learn) • Video clips, editorials, pictures • Journal writing • Experiments • Provocative questions • Problem/issue • Mysteries • Weird fact
INSTRUCTIONAL PROCESSES, APPLICATION, AND PRACTICE *help students move toward independent practice*	What teaching strategies and instructional tasks can help students achieve the objective?	• Whole group: brief lecture, demonstration, questioning, discussion, practice/review activities, "Model-Coach-Fade" approach • Small group: pair shares, cooperative learning
ASSESSMENT *determine attainment of lesson objective*	How will you know if students have met the objective?	• Informal: questioning, observation • Formal: quiz, written activities, final products
CLOSURE *bring the concepts of the lesson together*	How can the student express what was learned through the lesson?	• The L of a KWL • Exit card questions

It is important to realize that lessons are not entities of themselves. They are generally part of units, a structure recognized as an integral piece for helping students make meaningful connections. Units, in turn, are part of long-range plans, a structure that attends to year-long goals as they relate to state and diocesan standards. It is beyond the scope of this brief introduction to the topic of time in the classroom to cover these areas but nonetheless it remains important for the teacher to realize how a lesson is sequenced in the scope of learning—that is, to be attentive to the questions: Where does the lesson fit in relation to other lessons? What prerequisite skills and knowledge must the students master in order to successfully achieve the current lesson objective? What must follow the current lesson to build upon it in a logical way? These questions are critical in the ongoing process of planning.

Examples in Action

- Writing lesson objectives that use clear language and observable verbs, and are appropriate to student developmental level; choosing activities and assessments to match the objective.

- Incorporating a variety of activities; organizing them in a logical sequence with explicit connectors.

- Keeping lectures brief; enhancing them with visuals, demonstrations, and pair exchanges.

- Using examples and activities that connect learning with life beyond the classroom; making real world connections whenever possible.

- Making notes on what went well and what didn't in a lesson. These notes will help to inform follow-up lessons and will be very valuable in planning for a following year.

- Organizing a binder for each course taught to keep lesson plans and created materials.

Lesson Implementation

In terms of the actual lessons themselves, a teacher needs to utilize all available instructional minutes to full advantage. In any school situation, some things are beyond a teacher's control such as intercom announcements, fire drills, and absenteeism. In the classroom however, the utilization of instructional minutes is a factor that teachers directly control. Filling minutes is not enough because instructional time can be wasted if activities are not well chosen. Teachers must choose lesson activities and instructional tasks carefully so that minutes are used in the best possible manner.

In some estimates, as much as 30% of class time is taken up for non-instructional tasks (Stronge, 2007). These might include taking attendance, searching for materials or fiddling with equipment while students wait. Other times, lessons might end early with closing minutes left unstructured. In either case, it is easy to see how lesson minutes that are not fully utilized can add up over time.

There is one additional area in which minutes can get lost and that is when teachers need to interrupt the lesson to manage student behavior or address student inattention. Strong, engaging lesson plans help address both of these areas.

Examples in Action

- Organizing all needed lesson materials in advance of the start of the lesson.

- Choosing lesson activities and instructional tasks that develop the lesson's objective and are at an appropriate level of difficulty for the students.

- Reducing wasted minutes by having a plan in place if a lesson ends early; indicating to students what to do upon the completion of an exam.

- Obtaining the schedule for planned assemblies and events such as Christmas pageants and academic fairs at the start of the school year. In this way, teachers can consider these events when planning.

- Planning to celebrate a special event such as Catholic Schools Week by making connections of the theme to academic content.

Attention to pacing and transitions are also important in lesson implementation as they greatly affect momentum. Pacing is defined as the rate at which a teacher engages students in learning activities. Transitions are times during which the lesson moves between segments or activities, or the time between switching lessons. When both are effective, there are no instructional delays and no wasted class time.

Examples in Action

Pacing

- Being attentive to cues provided by students (facial expressions, off-task behavior).
- Varying activities at least every 8 to 12 minutes.
- Being organized with materials needed for the lesson and ordering them appropriately so that time is not wasted looking for items when needed.
- Maintaining a moderately brisk instructional pace. which is likely to hold student interest and attention when instruction is at the appropriate level of difficulty.

Transitions

- Posting the lesson agenda so that students can see the lesson's expectations.
- Using transitional statements between activities to link them and make them obvious to students (We have just listed what we know about Abraham Lincoln, let's list ideas about what you want to learn…).
- Informing students of the time allotted for a particular activity and using a timer to monitor the time.
- Using some sort of item (chimes, clicker, bell, rain stick) to signal a transition.
- Practicing any movement required between activities so that over time such movement occurs quickly and efficiently.
- Having sponge activities ready. Sponge activities include intriguing problems, mysteries, puzzles, prompts, and reinforcement activities that can be given to students when lessons finish early and there is extra class time. Having such handouts prepared and kept in a file can facilitate their use as needed.
- Planning alternative activities should there be a need for restructuring the lesson if content seems to be beyond students' current capabilities or should there be a need for refocusing students if they are not able to handle a less structured activity.
- Modeling for students an effective use of transition time. If a teacher wastes time searching for lesson handouts, students are given a message that the lesson is not ready to begin and might take advantage of the minutes for talking. Preparation and immediate engagement between lessons and lesson activities help to hold student attention.

High School Teaching

It seems that when I have all of my students engaged, the lesson goes beautifully with little disturbances. When my lesson doesn't quite flow, or I get stuck in a "rut" of doing the same types of activities day in and day out, students get bored and restless, and the trouble starts. So I have found that first, I must make a predictable routine regarding how the class begins and ends, and what is expected. Next, I have to offer a variety of activities that engage all different types of students.   — *Annie Walorski Morin*

Every moment is a teaching moment. We all know that there are times when students didn't do the homework that the day's lesson depends on, or a school assembly went overtime so you only have 15 minutes instead of 50. But there is always something to teach them, even if it is something to reinforce a procedure or practice. Engage students in a conversation about some topic you are covering, or about something in another class. Relate current events back to the material you are reading to help highlight its relevance to their lives. We have an obligation to use every moment we have with our students well; they pay a lot of money for this education, and each moment is a precious opportunity to help form our students.   — *Matt Reichert*

Middle School Teaching

I use a homework system based on completion and effort since not all students get support at home; however, I occasionally collect and grade their homework to make sure they are doing their best on the assignment. This system is quick and can be completed while students are working on their bell work. I give a 10/10 or 100% if it is all complete and they have followed the directions. I give a lower grade of 7/10 if more than a question or two is missing which signifies a C. I have students re-do the assignment if it is less than 80% completed for a late grade. Another important strategy is to borrow ideas, tips, worksheets, strategies, and projects from colleagues and former teachers to help lighten your workload. Try to have at least one great lesson in each of your classes once a week; this may not seem like a lot, but it will save heartache and keep your morale high instead of being disappointed and burned out after one semester of teaching.   — *Rory Dippold*

I find that the entire class runs smoothly if transitions and scheduling are consistent. Write your objectives for the day on the board. Vocalize the objectives at the beginning of each class period. Keep your schedule on the board so that the students know where you are in the class period. At the end of the period use a ticket out, consistently, to check how well the students accomplished the objective for the day.
    — *Lauren Flynn*

Transition is key. You need to be able to transition smoothly between activities, lessons, and subjects. Obviously, you need to have these specific lessons and activities preplanned, but there is so much more. Distribution of materials needs to be done quickly. There also needs to be some type of bell work that allows students to easily transition between lessons. Poor transitioning will allow students to lose focus, and it will become that much more difficult to get them refocused. Good transitioning just takes practice, so do not feel badly if it does not initially work well.   — *Brett Guy*

Bell work might seem like an insignificant part of lesson plans; however, it is essential. If students immediately begin working on a question related to the previous class or to their own lives, it sets the tone for a productive class period.

— *Laura Farrell*

In math class, I like to find a few difficult problems for students to complete when they finish the assigned problems in class. Quietly giving the students a challenging problem pushes them to continue working effectively while providing other students with time to finish their assigned problems and ask questions.

— *Anna Arias*

Elementary School Teaching

If students finished their work early, they would have "challenge packets" in their seatwork folders for them to do. These challenge packets would have seasonal activities as well as extra work in math, English, writing, and spelling/phonics. The work in the challenge packets would include review work and also work that might be slightly ahead of grade level or where we were in our lessons. I also had educational centers in manila envelopes in the back of the room that they could take to their seat when they finished their work. These centers would always review work that we had already covered in class. They mainly worked on reading skills and phonics and social studies.

— *Katie Cawley*

No matter what the interruption is during the day, do your best to stick to your timetable. If there is a 20 minute interruption during math...just go on to the next lesson as per timetable. The students need to see consistency and they like to know what comes next. Make sure you have the day's schedule posted on the board at the start of the day. It's nice to give each child a copy of the timetable and even have them set the schedule for the next day (taking turns to follow the timetable).

— *Heather Barker*

In reading, I have portions each day. First, we do a mini-class lesson. One example is finding the main idea. Then, we have guided reading and centers. I have four groups each week. One is always guided reading. The other groups vary depending on the week. In my Listening Center, the students listen to and follow along with a book on tape/CD and complete an activity. In my Word Work Center, the students work on phonics or making words activities. In the Readers' Theater, the students work for 4 weeks to: practice their parts, complete an activity, make a prop, and perform. In the Author Study Center, students read a book from one author, such as Mark Teague (I pick up several books from the library) and complete an activity. I also have a writing center.

— *Courtney Jianas Vogtner*

Having a reading corner is important. Students can go there when they finish work early. In our reading corner we had chapter books, but I'd also go to the library and get books pertaining to what we were learning in science and social studies as well as books I knew the students would enjoy. In the reading corner there were also math and division flash cards and Brainquest, know your states, and know your presidents games. The students loved the area so much that when we had indoor recess they all played with the things over there instead of gabbing with friends or drawing on the chalkboard. It was really neat to see them wanting to learn together.

— *Brynn Johnson*

A quiet classroom is not a learning classroom (especially in science). I'm a firm believer that if the students aren't moving, handling, exploring, discussing, debating . . . they aren't learning.

— *Patrick Vogtner*

REFERENCES

Aronson, J., Zimmerman, J., & Carlos, L. (1998). *Improving student achievement by extending school: Is it just a matter of time?* Retrieved November 23, 2009, from http://www.wested.org/cs/we/view/rs/95

Aronson, J., Zimmerman, J., & Carlos, L. (2001). *Making time count.* Retrieved November 23, 2009, from http://www.wested.org/cs/we/view/rs/535

Bloom B. S. (Ed.). (1956). *Taxonomy of educational cbjectives, the classification of educational goals. Handbook I: Cognitive domain.* New York: McKay.

Congregation for Catholic Education. (1997). *The Catholic school on the threshold of the third millennium.* Rome: Libreria Editrice Vaticana.

Congregation for Catholic Education. (1988). *The religious dimension of education in a Catholic school.* Washington, DC: United States Catholic Conference.

Cotton, K. (2000). *The schooling practices that matter most.* Alexandria, VA: Association for Supervision and Curriculum Development.

Drake, S., & Burns, R. (2004). *Meeting standards through integrated curriculum.* Alexandria, VA: Association for Supervision and Curriculum Development.

Fisher, D. (2009). The use of instructional time in the typical high school classroom. *Educational Forum, 73*(2), 168-176.

Grolund, N. (2004). *Writing instructional objectives for teaching and assessment.* Upper Saddle River, NJ: Pearson Education.

Jensen, E. (2005). *Teaching with the brain in mind* (2nd ed.). Alexandria: Association for Supervision and Curriculum Development.

McGeehan, J. (2001). Brain-compatible learning. *Green Teacher, 64,* 7-12.

Miller, J. M. (2006). *The Holy See's teaching on Catholic schools.* Atlanta, GA: Solidarity Association.

Pashler, H., Bain, P., Bottge, B., Graesser, A., Koedinger, K., McDaniel, M., & Metcalfe, J. (2007). *Organizing instruction and study to improve student learning* (NCER 2007-2004). Washington, DC: National Center for Education Research, Institute of Education Sciences, U.S. Department of Education. Retrieved from http://ncer.ed.gov.

Roth, K., & Garnier, H. (2006). What science teaching looks like: An international perspective. *Educational Leadership, 64*(4), 16-23.

Stronge, J. (2007). *Qualities of effective teachers* (2nd ed.). Alexandria, VA: Association for Supervision and Curriculum Development.

Wiggins, G., & McTighe, J. (1998). *Understanding by design.* Alexandria, VA: Association for Supervision and Curriculum Development.

Wolfe, P. (2001). *Brain matters: Translating research into classroom practice.* Alexandria, VA: Association for Supervision and Curriculum Development.

Zimmerman, J. (2001). How much does time affect learning? *Principal, 80*(3), 6-11.

TEMPLATES

WRITING LESSON OBJECTIVES

Cognitive Process of Bloom's Taxonomy	Verbs		Sample Objectives (Students Will Be Able To...)
KNOWLEDGE	define identify label list	match name recall reproduce	SWBAT list salient characteristics of the Elizabethan theater. (H) SWBAT name the Ten Commandments. (E)
COMPREHENSION	describe discuss explain illustrate	interpret paraphrase summarize translate	SWBAT describe major economic and social trends of the late 20th century. (H) SWBAT explain how fossil/rock evidence supports the theory of continental drift. (M)
APPLICATION	calculate construct predict prepare	produce project solve use	SWBAT find the perimeter of a rectangle. (E) SWBAT apply the law of conservation of energy to a swinging pendulum conceptually and mathematically. (H)
ANALYSIS	analyze break down connect compare	contrast debate distinguish separate	SWBAT compare and contrast citizenship in ancient Athens and Sparta. (M) SWBAT analyze the relationship between plot and conflict within a short story. (M)
SYNTHESIS	combine compose create design	invent modify plan revise	SWBAT create a two-dimensional composition that demonstrates knowledge and appropriate use of principles of design (repetition, scale, proportion, emphasis, rhythm, unity, and/or harmony). (M) SWBAT compose an original short story. (E)
EVALUATION	appraise assess conclude evaluate	judge justify rank rate	SWBAT critique a famous work of art using appropriate terminology and elements and principles of design. (H) Evaluate the credibility of a web site using given criteria. (M)

CHOOSING APPROPRIATE ASSESSMENTS
AND TEACHING/LEARNING STRATEGIES

Cognitive Process of Bloom's Taxonomy	Appropriate Assessments	Useful Teaching/Learning Strategies
KNOWLEDGE	Tests Quizzes Orations of famous speeches	Notetaking Mnemonics, vocabulary cards Linking activities Games, tournaments
COMPREHENSION	Essays Projects Charts Diagrams Collages	Concept mapping Use of graphic organizers, schematic diagrams, charts, analogies
APPLICATION	Projects Constructions Written products Solutions to problems and steps used to solve them	Flow charts Outlines of process steps Steps to problem solving Process writing Learning centers Simulation activities
ANALYSIS	Data analysis of research Graph analysis Debates	Research projects Conducting surveys, investigations, experiments Venn diagrams
SYNTHESIS	Original writings: poems, articles, plays Inventions Musical compositions	Use of figurative language Summarizing from research Analogies
EVALUATION	Position papers Critiques Conclusions drawn from experiments and/or research	Activities that require making a recommendation based upon given criteria Use of criteria checklists and rating scales to assess products (a web site, articles, etc.)

ORGANIZATIONAL AIDS

K (What I Know)	**W** (What I Want to Know)	**L** (What I Learned)

ANTICIPATION GUIDE

Note to teacher: Add ideas to the "statement" column that invite student opinion or activate prior knowledge regarding the topic under study. At the end of the lesson (or after reading assigned text), ask students to go back to the Guide to revisit each statement and complete the "After" column.

Directions: Read each statement and place a check in the "Before" column if you agree with the statement or a minus if you disagree with it. Be prepared to discuss.

Before	Statement	After

CONCEPT MAP WITH SPACE FOR NOTES

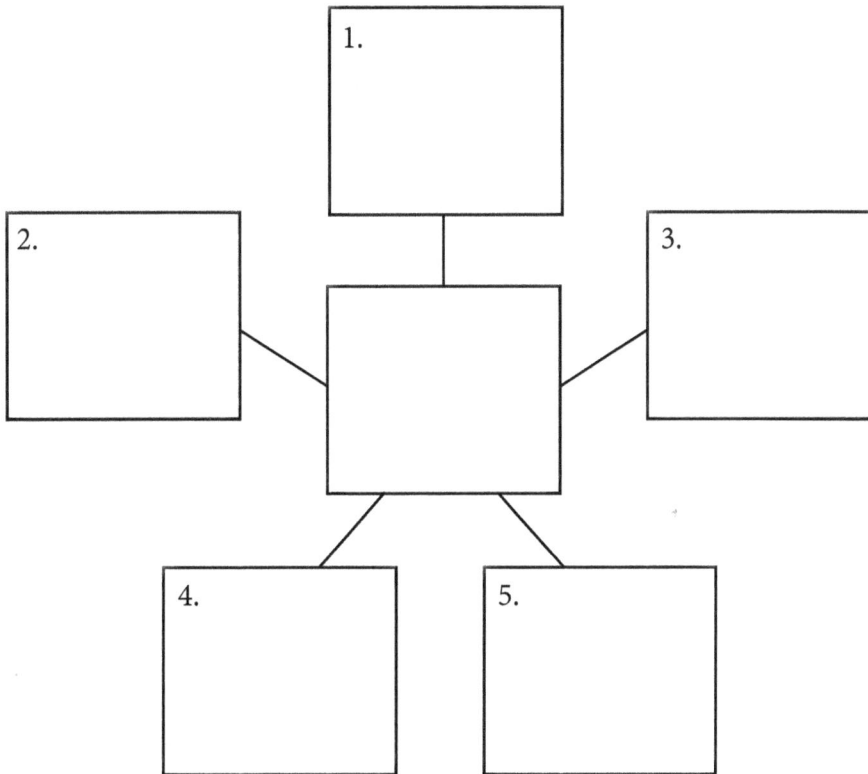

1.

2.

3.

4.

5.

1.

2.

3.

4.

5.

CREATING YOUR MANAGEMENT PLAN
Classroom Time

Reflect upon important considerations for spending classroom time well and jot down ideas related to each of the following questions.

1. Miller (2006) writes that a mark of a Catholic school is that it is imbued with a Catholic worldview throughout its curriculum. What is your understanding of this statement? How will your instructional planning reflect this idea?
2. Generate a list of ways instructional time could be interrupted in your classroom. For each item listed, think of a concrete way to address it.

3. Obtain a copy of your state or diocesan standards. Take time to familiarize yourself with all that is stated. Choose one of the outcomes and develop a lesson using the following process:
   a. Determine lesson objective: What will students know and be able to do by the end of the lesson?
   b. Choose assessment: How will it be determined that students have achieved the objective?
   c. Decide teaching strategies: What teaching strategies and instructional tasks can help students achieve the objective?

Grading and Communication

Ongoing communication is an essential aspect of building relationships and strengthening community, both of which support student learning. Though communication with all constituents needs to be ongoing, parents—as the primary educators of their children—deserve special attention. When parents are kept informed, they are invited into an active partnership with educators to support the learning of their child.

There are many means for communication and these include telephone calls, newsletters, e-mail updates, class web pages, impromptu meetings, parent-teacher conferences, and open houses as common methods. Another usual means of communication is through grade reports. Grading is a necessary part of teaching that serves many purposes. Grades provide students and their parents information about progress and achievement, are used for administrative reasons to determine such things as credits for graduation, and may also serve a role in motivation and guidance (Airasian, 2001). Each of these uses for grades reveals a common reality: grading serves an important role in communication and none more important than providing information about academic progress to parents and to the students themselves.

- Frequent assessment and timely feedback positively impacts student achievement. Feedback that most benefits learners is encouraging and provides clear information about progress and how to improve (Marzano, 2006).

- Parental involvement is associated with higher student achievement. This is true for students of all ages and for families from all racial/ethnic, educational and socio-economic backgrounds (Henderson & Mapp, 2002; Jeynes, 2005).

- Parent involvement reflecting academic socialization has a strong positive association with middle school student achievement (Hill & Tyson, 2009). Academic socialization includes such things as "communicating parental expectations for education and its value or utility, linking schoolwork to current events, fostering educational and occupational aspirations, discussing learning strategies with children, and making preparations and plans for the future" (p. 742).

- Catholic school parents are more involved than public school parents despite having fewer formal opportunities for school involvement (Mulligan, 2003).

CONSIDERATIONS FOR GRADING

To engage in a process of making valid and reliable judgments, a teacher must accumulate evidence of learning that is varied in form and sufficient in representation.

Many questions are worthy of consideration for establishing valid grading practices and three will be discussed: (1) What shall be included in a grade average? (2) How will academic evidence be weighted? (3) How should grades be monitored?

What Shall Be Included in a Grade Average?

Grading is a process of making judgments about student performance. A teacher can make judgments in relation to many areas: achievement, effort, motivation, attitude, and conduct. Even though judgments can be made in all of these areas, it doesn't mean that they all should be included in grade averages. Grades should reflect academic performance.

There are two categories that should be considered in a grading schema: achievement grades and effort-based grades. Achievement grades relate to assessments that students complete individually and independently to show their attainment of goals and/or objectives. These assessments include tests, quizzes, and projects/performance assessments. Effort-based grades relate to assignments that show a completion of tasks—class work, bell work, homework—and expectations for participation. These effort-based grades might very well show achievement but they are less easily and less accurately measured. Take homework, for example. It is difficult to determine if completed homework truly reflects the work of the student. Did a parent help? To what degree? Did two students work together to complete their homework? It might be equally hard to grade participation. How is the participation defined? Is it the completion of written work during a lesson? Is it a tally of questions answered? Is it participation in a small group activity? Because there is less clarity with the effort-based grades, the majority of a student's grade should be weighted to reflect achievement as noted through individually and independently completed assessments.

The "Achievement/Effort Ratio" chart (see Table 3) suggests percentages for weighting achievement and effort to determine a grading average. Generally, achievement is weighted more and effort less as students progress from elementary school to high school. As an example, a third grade teacher might utilize a 55/45 achievement/effort ratio; a high school teacher might utilize a 70/30 achievement/effort ratio.

Table 3. *Achievement/Effort Ratio in Grade Averages*

	Elementary School	Middle School	High School
Achievement Grades *Tests, Quizzes, Projects, Performance Assessments*	55-60%	60-65%	65-75%
Effort-Based Grades *Homework, Bell work, Class work, Participation*	45-40%	40-35%	35-25%

Motivation, attitude, and conduct are significant factors that impact student learning. They do not accurately reflect academic performance, however, and therefore, their inclusion in grading averages is not appropriate. Rather, most report cards and progress reports are designed to include separate categories for noting such things.

How Will Evidence Be Weighted?

A second question of significance is how will evidence of learning be weighted within a specific course/subject grade? If there are grading categories that include tests, quizzes, projects/performance assessments, homework, participation, and class work, how much will each of these areas be worth?

A teacher must consider the weighting of categories very carefully. First, the total weights of tests, quizzes, projects/performance assessments to the total weights of homework, participation, and class work should match the achievement to effort ratio previously determined. Second, it is important to anticipate a reasonable number of assessments that will be given throughout a marking period. For example, is it fair to weight tests at 40% of a grade and only provide one test?

Sample Weighting of Grades

HIGH SCHOOL

Sample 1: English		*Sample 2: Math*		*Sample 3: Foreign Language*	
Tests/Essays	60%	Tests	40%	Tests/Performance assessments	40%
Quizzes	15%	Quizzes	25%	Quizzes	25%
Homework	15%	Homework	15%	Class work	25%
Class work	10%	In-class work	20%	Homework	10%

MIDDLE SCHOOL

Sample 1: Social Studies		*Sample 2: Language Arts*		*Sample 3: Science*	
Tests/Projects	40%	Tests	25%	Tests	30%
Quizzes	20%	Papers/Essays/Projects	25%	Quizzes	25%
Homework	15%	Quizzes	15%	Labs	10%
Daily work	15%	Homework	15%	Homework	20%
Participation/Binder checks	10%	Daily language practice	20%	Bell work/Participation	15%

ELEMENTARY SCHOOL

Sample 1: Grade 5		*Sample 2: Grade 3*		*Sample 3: Grade 2*	
Tests/Projects	40%	Tests/Performance assessments	40%	Tests/Projects	40%
Quizzes	20%	Quizzes	15%	Quizzes	15%
Daily opening work	10%	Homework	15%	Homework	15%
Class work	15%	Class work	20%	Class work	15%
Homework	15%	Journal	10%	Participation	15%

What Is the Best Way to Monitor Grades?

The best way to monitor grades is to keep averages current. In this way you will be in a better position to evaluate learning, keep parents informed with accurate information, and provide timely feedback to students.

Grading is time consuming and teachers are busy with many responsibilities. For this reason, it is helpful to utilize efficient grading practices to review work and record grades. A computerized grading program offers many benefits for monitoring grades. Programs will allow grade categories to be weighted and averages calculated in an ongoing way so that at anytime, a student grade can be known. Another advantage is that statistics can be easily calculated providing a teacher valuable data for analyzing performances.

Many school systems have computerized grading programs that they require their teachers to use, and some of these have online capabilities allowing for immediate and ongoing access by parents and the students themselves. If a school does not provide a computerized grading program, a spreadsheet program or a prepackaged grading program might be used.

Examples in Action

To review work:

- Setting aside time each day to grade. The more timely the feedback, the more meaningful it is to students and the more motivating it is for ongoing learning.
- Always collecting work that you tell students you will collect. This increases likelihood of completion and quality.
- Reviewing homework for neat, complete, and organized. A three-point system (3 for neat, complete and organized, 1 or 2 for incomplete work, 0 for no work) might work well.
- Occasionally collecting homework and reviewing for accuracy.
- Reviewing more subjective types of achievement tasks—projects, essays, and other performance assessments—using a rubric. Rubrics are instruments with specified criteria and scales for rating student work. Multiple ready-made rubrics and rubric generators are available on the Internet and can be easily adapted to meet one's specific needs.

To record grades:

- Keeping grade averages up-to-date so that they accurately reflect current student achievement.
- Backing up computerized grade books so that grades are never lost.
- Displaying care when communicating grades so that confidentiality is maintained.
- Being aware that some schools require that grades be shared with parents as percents. Check with your schools to learn of grading expectations.

CONSIDERATIONS FOR PARENT/GUARDIAN COMMUNICATION

As research shows, parent involvement has a positive impact on student achievement. Finding ways to communicate with parents and involve them in their child's education are important endeavors. At all levels of education, parents appreciate communication.

Students come from a variety of backgrounds and many factors may influence parent involvement. It is important to assume that all parents want what is best for their child and it is unfair to pass judgment on how that desire is shown. Language difficulties, work commitments, and a variety of other factors could be involved when a parent is unable to attend various school functions or appears non-responsive to a teacher's specific requests. It is a teacher's responsibility to find ways to reach out to parents and to work with them. The utilization of varied communication practices is important.

"Parents have a particularly important part to play in the educating community, since it is to them that primary and natural responsibility for their children's education belongs. Unfortunately in our day there is a widespread tendency to delegate this unique role. Therefore it is necessary to foster initiatives which encourage commitment, but which provide at the same time the right sort of concrete support which the family needs and which involve it in the Catholic school's educational project.(26) The constant aim of the school therefore, should be contact and dialogue with the pupils' families, which should also be encouraged through the promotion of parents' associations, in order to clarify with their indispensable collaboration that personalized approach which is needed for an educational project to be efficacious" (Congregation for Catholic Education [CCE], 1997, §20).

To Develop and Maintain Good Relationships

There are a number of communication practices that can be helpful for developing relationships. Brief notes, telephone calls, or e-mails can be used to recognize student achievement or positive behavior. Invitations to attend a special Mass, academic fair, or cultural event can express welcome. Weekly letters, monthly newsletters, or a class web page can inform parents of classroom happenings and provide helpful resources. Unexpected meetings at school sporting and social events or greeting parents at dismissal can provide opportunities for a friendly exchange and a positive comment to be expressed.

Establishing solid parent-teacher relationships through practices such as these supports student learning and facilitates any discussions for behavioral or academic concerns should they need to occur.

Examples in Action

- Starting the communication process early. Using introductory letters or newsletters to outline expectations, grading scale, and information you want shared.

- Making calls/sending e-mails for positive reasons (behavior, academics, a quality displayed, effort shown, etc.).

- Providing monthly newsletters and/or weekly notices about what is occurring in the classroom, even including dates for upcoming tests and/or due dates for specific assignments (appropriate in the elementary and middle school grades).

- Maintaining a class web site noting homework assignments, anticipated test dates, and helpful links for parents and students.

- Inviting parents to the classroom for special presentations or to view displayed work and projects (appropriate in the elementary grades).

- Involving parents in the school as mystery readers and aides (in the elementary classroom), as guest speakers and chaperones (at all grade levels).

To Communicate Grades

As previously noted, grades provide information about student achievement. Schools vary in grading practices but generally provide three or four grade reports annually.

Outside of official grade reports, try to provide frequent communication about grades, and missing or incomplete work. If a student is falling behind, a low report card grade should not be the first indicator about struggles.

To Communicate Concerns

It is possible that a teacher will need to reach out to parents because of a behavioral or academic concern (i.e., a pattern of misbehavior or a single incident of blatant disrespect or defiance; a series of missing or incomplete homework assignments, low quiz grades, or accumulated evidence of ongoing struggles). In the event that this needs to occur, involve parents early. A telephone call or e-mail message can be helpful to address specific needs. Should a situation warrant additional attention, a parent-teacher conference might be appropriate.

Parent-teacher conferences are formally scheduled by the school and typically occur at the end of a marking term. They can also be requested by either parent or teacher for specific concerns. No matter who initiates the conference or its purpose, there are a number of practices that help to facilitate productive interactions: providing a warm welcome, maintaining a professional demeanor (polite language, respectful attitudes), presenting data to substantiate comments (test scores, number of tardies), and offering positive statements (about the student, the meeting itself, and future actions to be taken).

"The more the members of the educational community develop a real willingness to collaborate among themselves, the more fruitful their work will be. Achieving the educational aims of the school should be an equal priority for teachers, students and families alike, each one according to his or her own role, always in the Gospel spirit of freedom and love. Therefore channels of communication should be open among all those concerned with the school. Frequent meetings will help to make this possible, and a willingness to discuss common problems candidly will enrich this communication" (CCE, 1988, §38).

Examples in Action

- Maintaining a professional demeanor at all times when communicating with parents. This should be reflected in manner of dress, speech, and written comments.

- Beginning any communication with a positive statement about the student.

- Providing documentation to substantiate specific comments made. Samples of student work, a list of missing assignments, behavioral incidents that have been documented, number of tardies/absences, etc.

- Maintaining focus on the student being discussed with his/her parents and not revealing any information about other students.

- Maintaining a log of all parent communications that documents date and reason for contact.

TIPS AND IDEAS FROM THE FIELD

High School Teaching

Make it your goal to contact parents about "good things" at least every time you contact a parent about a "bad thing." All too often parents only receive phone calls or e-mails from teachers when something is wrong. It's important to keep parents informed, but they should know about all of the good stuff, too. Call home when they get a perfect score on a quiz, or when they show some strong interest in a particular subject, or when they have been struggling with some concept and finally had a breakthrough. Communication is incredibly important for so many things—classroom management, academic/behavioral concerns, parent support of teacher/school procedures and rules—but it is also important for reinforcing students in what they already do well, or areas where they are improving.

— *Matt Reichert*

Always record any communication you have with a parent. Make communication with the parents early and often, especially if you feel that the student might end up needing some extra attention for one reason or another down the road. This early intervention on your part will more easily win the parent to your perspective on the situation and will garner a spirit of teamwork. — *Noah Beacom*

I found it helpful to check class work (worksheets/notes) for completion and made that worth 25% of the class grade. This motivated students to use their time wisely.   — *Michelle Blair*

Middle School Teaching

Start off the year with a positive phone call home to each student (if possible). Really look for specific, meaningful details about a student that you can compliment. Build a strong relationship with the parents as early as possible, letting them know that you are there and you care!   — *Lauren Flynn*

If possible, contact all the parents of the students' you have before the "Back to School" night; however, if time is limited contact the most at-risk students' parents. Building a strong and positive relationship early in the year will help you start building rapport. This measure will also make you feel more comfortable when you meet with parents the night of "Back to School." I try and make it a point to send a "Good News" referral or a positive e-mail once a day to a different parent. This can really make a parent and student's day! At the beginning of the year, have parents fill out a detailed form with their name (last name may be different), address, e-mail, work, home and if possible cell phone number. In case of emergencies or a need to contact parents, you do not need to go to the office for the information. This can also be accomplished by having the students do it the first day of class on an index card.   — *Rory Dippold*

Make an index card with each child's name and contact information on it. Every time you communicate with parents/guardians, write it on the back on the card. For example, 9/2-introduction; 9/10-first week update; 10/1-missing project concerns; 10/5-grading update; 10/6-behavior concern; 11/5-positive feedback. If anything is going to escalate, you have strict documentation of what you did and when. This is great back-up for you any time behavior or academics is an area of concern. It shows that you did your part.   — *Matt Houlihan*

I recommend that you run the first e-mails or letters that you send home by your principal or vice principal. I failed to realize that my principal needed to okay my first letter home, and I had to make copies again of all the letters. Also, my vice principal had wonderful ideas on how to improve my e-mails.   — *Anna Arias*

Stay on top of things! You need to get grading done in a timely manner, as this lets the students have immediate feedback on their work and progress. This also provides the teacher with direct knowledge of the students' progress, and this knowledge can be communicated effectively to parents if a student is falling behind in a subject. Send home praise notes or place phone calls if a student starts doing well in a subject that previously caused them problems (or starts behaving when they previously caused discipline issues). Oftentimes, these parents just hear about the bad things, and it really makes their day (and the student's day) when they hear about the good. This can also provide the student with additional reinforcement to keep up the good work.   — *Brett Guy*

As one of my glaring weaknesses, mention of grading gives me a queasy feeling. It can be likened to balancing a checkbook or another tedious, necessary task that sometimes reveals unpleasant news. I think it's important to remind oneself of the meaning behind grades; an assessment of student progress. As difficult as it may be, the more frequently students and parents receive feedback, the better. Eventually, the goal is to communicate to students that grades are their responsibility, not just an arbitrary letter. If students keep a portfolio of important assignments/tests from each quarter, they can personally keep track of their grades and be graded on their overall improvement at the end of the year. Averaging one's test, homework, and quiz grade can be incorporated into a math lesson and encouraged for all classes. When communicating to a large number of parents during conferences, I print out a grade summary for each student that breaks down grades into categories (tests/quizzes, etc.) It's a simple way to speak to the areas in which each student excels and areas in which they may improve.

— *Laura Farrell*

Elementary School Teaching

Be completely open about everything. The best way to do that is by having a mandatory beginning of the year parent-teacher meeting. I have a monthly e-newsletter that goes out called "The Peek At The Month," that gives parents an idea of what we will be doing as a class during that month. In addition to that, I have daily assignments explained in detail on our class web site. In addition to that, I have a class blog that posts resources that my students can use. It is all about covering your bases as much as possible.

— *C.J. Egalite*

I try to communicate with parents as frequently as I can. One of the best ways I have found to do this is through the student planners. At the beginning of the year I let parents know that this is a great way to reach me. Little notes like, "great day today, no homework turned in, or don't forget PE tomorrow," go a long way. They are an easy way to reach parents and help to keep a record of ongoing communication.

— *Clare Murphy*

I tried to begin the year by calling home to each student's parents with at least one positive comment. This initially uplifting conversation paved the way for a constructive parent-teacher relationship and made future calls much easier to make and more thoughtfully received.

— *Lindsay Fitzpatrick*

In order to ensure that I sent a positive note home to a student's parents at least one time per semester, I would address the note card and envelope to the parents at the beginning of each semester. I would keep these cards accessible on my desk. Anytime I saw a student doing something outstanding that was worthy of writing home to tell the parents, I would have the note cards there ready and waiting!

— *Katie Cawley*

Many teachers communicate to parents when students' grades are in danger, but try to do the opposite too! Sometimes, when students did unexpectedly well, I would let them make a special phone call home and they loved it!

— *Maya Noronha*

I sent home monthly parent newsletters with updates about academics, procedural changes, field trips, and other classroom news. You could also use these newsletters as a chance to give the parents information about how to apply for a public library card for their child (many will never have done that before!), offer prayers that can be said at home, and give parents other suggestions for how to connect their child's school and home lives. I also sent home a weekly "Test Notice" that informed parents of the upcoming tests, quizzes, and projects. These test notices had to be signed and returned each week, and I knew that parents had advance warning for all the major assignments coming up.

— *Amy Bozzo*

Keep the parents informed of each child's progress. Have each child get a folder with a sheet in it that has the week and weeks of the year laid out (like a calendar) and two columns—one for grades and the other for behavior. Call a meeting with parents to talk about a child's improvement or in concern of consistently poor grades. Print out averages every month for the parents to see overall progress.

— *Heather Barker*

The best thing I ever did was to put up a free website by Google. I can post notes, forms, upcoming assessments, videos, supplemental websites, and more. It gave the students every opportunity to succeed in the class and took away every excuse from both parents and students. — *Patrick Vogtner*

I ask for parent volunteers at the beginning of the year. This form is attached to my handbook.

Classroom Parent Helper's Name _____

Child's Name _____

Phone Number _____ E-mail _____

Please circle any ways you are willing to help and return as soon as possible. I will contact you if I will need your help.

1. I would like to donate disposable cameras for the class to take photos throughout the year.
2. I am willing to develop photos from the disposable cameras.
3. I am willing to chaperone a class field trip.
4. I would like to help cut out letters for bulletin boards or decorate a bulletin board.
5. I will help find supplies or be in charge of finding supplies for classroom projects and/or experiments.
6. I would be willing to help a small group during a class project.
7. I am willing to donate small/inexpensive prizes (stickers, candy, bookmarks, erasers, stamps, bubbles, little toys, etc. under $1) for our Good Behavior Lottery.
8. I am willing to present about _____
9. Other_____

— *Courtney Jianas Vogtner*

REFERENCES

Airasian, P. (2001). *Classroom assessment: Concepts and applications.* Boston: McGraw-Hill.

Congregation for Catholic Education. (1997). *The Catholic school on the threshold of the third millennium.* Rome: Libreria Editrice Vaticana.

Congregation for Catholic Education. (1988). *The religious dimension of education in a Catholic school.* Washington, DC: United States Catholic Conference.

Jeynes, W. (2005). *Parental involvement and student achievement: A meta-analysis.* Retrieved from http://www.gse.harvard.edu/hfrp/projects/fine/resources/digest/meta.html

Henderson, A., & Mapp, K. (2002). *A new wave of evidence: The impact of school, family, and community connections on student achievement.* Southwest Educational Development Laboratory. Retrieved from http: www.sedl.org/connections/

Hill, N., & Tyson, D. (2009). Parental involvement in middle school: A meta-analytic assessment of the strategies that promote achievement. *Developmental Psychology, 45*(3), 740-763.

Marzano, R. (2006). *Classroom assessment and grading that work.* Alexandria, VA: Association for Supervision and Curriculum Development.

Mulligan, G. (2003). Sector differences in opportunities for parental involvement in the school context. *Catholic Education: A Journal of Inquiry and Practice, 7*(2), 246-265.

MISSING ASSIGNMENT NOTICE

Date: _____

Student: _____

Assignment: _____

_____

_____

Parent/Guardian Signature: _____

MISSING HOMEWORK NOTICE

Date: _____

I did not complete this homework assignment: _____
I have checked my consequence.
_____First missing assignment this quarter—parent notification
_____Second missing assignment this quarter—parent notification
_____Third missing assignment this quarter—30 minute stay after school on _____
_____More than three missing assignments—30 minute stay after school on _____

Student signature: _____

Teacher signature: _____

Parent signature and date: _____
Comments:

SAMPLE TEST NOTICE
Week of 9/19-9/23

This is a note to let you know what tests and projects are scheduled for this coming week. I will always send a test notice like this one home in your child's Monday Folder. I ask that you please sign the bottom of the notice and send it back with your child so that I know that you are aware of the upcoming tests. Please save the top portion of the notice and post it someplace visible in your home so that your child is aware of the upcoming tests and projects.

Monday 9/19 through Friday 9/23: Iowa Test of Basic Skills (make sure your child is eating breakfast and getting enough sleep!)

Wednesday 9/21: Religion quiz on worship chapter (Chapter 1)

Thursday 9/22: Student presentations on Mars

**There will be no Spelling this week due to the IOWA tests!

Thanks so much, and have a great week!

~ Miss _____

• •

Please cut on this line and return the bottom portion on Tuesday, 9/20.

I have read this Test Notice, and I am aware of the tests/projects for the week.

Parent's signature _____ Date _____

Child's signature _____ Date _____

WORK SAMPLES COVER SHEET

Included within this folder are the following graded work samples:

_____

_____

_____

_____

Please sign below to indicate you have received and reviewed all of the above assignments. If an assignment is missing, please let me know.

Comments/Questions:

_____

_____

_____

_____

Signature of parent/guardian: _____

KEEP ONE COPY OF THIS FORM. SIGN AND RETURN THE OTHER WITH ALL GRADED WORK. THE GRADED WORK IS NOT TO BE KEPT AT HOME.

PARENT COMMUNICATION DOCUMENTATION FORM

Date	Student Name	Person Contacted	Method E-mail Phone Meeting	Reason Behavior Grades Missing work Praise Tardies	Response

Reflect upon and answer the questions offered in this section.

1. What will be the ratio of achievement to effort grades in your grading schema?
2. How will academic evidence be weighted?
3. Will you have access to a grading program? If not, what is your plan for monitoring grades?
4. List ideas for developing and maintaining solid communication practices with parents.

Index

A

achievement/effort ratio 89
assertiveness 46, 48-49, 51-52
attendance 4, 25, 26, 35, 37, 75

B

Bloom's Taxonomy 71, 80, 81

C

Catholic classroom 3, 6, 8, 13-14, 19
Catholic culture for learning 3, 4
Catholic identity 3, 4, 6, 19
Christ-like atmosphere 4-5, 19
Church documents 3
classroom community 7, 48
classroom management 5, 23, 24, 45, 46, 47, 49
classroom space 4, 6, 19
communication 5, 46, 54, 87, 93-96, 105
community 3, 4, 5, 7, 9, 19, 20, 23, 24, 45, 48, 49, 87, 93, 95
consequences 34, 45-46, 49, 51-56, 57-59, 65
    negative 53-54, 65
    positive 56, 65
consistency 46, 49, 51, 57, 58, 78
curriculum alignment 69

D

disruptions 24, 46, 53, 57, 58
diversity 5, 47, 69, 70
documentation 96, 97, 104

E-F-G

Gospel values 6, 8, 45, 48, 50
grades
    achievement 88-89, 105
    communicating 94-95
    effort-based 88-89, 105
    monitoring 91, 105
    weighting 89, 90, 91, 105
grading 87-92, 105

H

housekeeping routines 32, 33

I

instructional planning 67, 68, 69, 84
instructional time 24, 68, 74, 84

J-K-L

learning styles 70
lesson implementation 67, 74, 75
lesson objectives 74, 80
liturgical year 10, 11-12

About the Author

Sister Gail Mayotte is Faculty and Coordinator of Supervision in the Alliance for Catholic Education Service through Teaching Program at the University of Notre Dame. A former teacher, principal, and diocesan curriculum and testing director, she holds a Ph.D. in Curriculum and Instruction from Boston College. She is the author of the book, *Prayers to Guide Teaching*, also published by ACE Press. Sister Gail is a member of the Congregation of the Sisters of the Assumption of the Blessed Virgin.

www.ingramcontent.com/pod-product-compliance
Lightning Source LLC
Chambersburg PA
CBHW081153090426

42736CB00017B/3305